Tales of
SOUTH WALES

Tales of
SOUTH WALES

WRITTEN BY
Ken Radford

FROM STORIES GATHERED
AND ILLUSTRATED BY
Schoolchildren of South Wales

WITH A FOREWORD BY
Wynford Vaughan-Thomas

SKILTON & SHAW
52 Lincoln's Inn Fields · London

© KEN RADFORD, 1979
ISBN 0 7050 0079 6 (hardback)
ISBN 0 7050 0080 X (limp)
Printed in Great Britain for
Skilton & Shaw (Fudge & Co., Ltd.),
Sardinia House, Sardinia Street, London WC2A 3NW
by Biddles Ltd., Martyr Road,
Guildford, Surrey, from text set by
Specialised Offset Services Limited, Liverpool

Contents

Foreword

Among its hills and valleys, across moorland and along its rugged coastline, South Wales abounds in tales of wonder and folk belief: tales of rogues and heroes, witches and the tylwyth teg (the fair folk), wreckers and rescuers; and stories of ghosts, both melancholy and fearful. In the 65 tales retold here, Ken Radford has gathered together the most comprehensive collection from these southern counties of Wales. It is refreshing to note that they are tales told as was originally intended – unpolished, in style similar to the 'chwedl' of old Welsh literature.

I am especially intrigued to learn how many of the stories were gathered orally by schoolchildren whose great-grandparents have recalled the tales told them at the fireside, long before the days of television and other modes of popular entertainment. Accounts of these anecdotes were written down and the candour and simplicity of the children's narrative is reflected in such tales as 'The Green Cwm', 'The Cellar', 'A Haunted Place' and 'Tales of Dwr Dirgelaidd'.

No collection of folklore from South Wales would be complete without such old favourites as the adventures of Twm Shon Cati, or the legends of Llyn Barfog, Llyn y Fan Fach and Devil's Bridge. These have been told and retold since time immemorial. And the courage of our rescuers, along the coasts and beneath the ground, will never be forgotten. *Tales of South Wales* recall these and a variety of others, many of which would have been forgotten in the years ahead. Among them are a number of original recollections related by the old folk of Dyfed, Powys, Glamorgan and Gwent, which the author has moulded into genuine short stories – 'The Devil of Bryn-y-Wrach', 'The Victors' Chariot', 'There was an Old Woman', 'True Love', 'Someone on the stairs' ...

I am confident that the collection will prove to be very popular and will bring a great deal of enjoyment to its readers – to the folk of South Wales, both young and old; to those with fond memories of Wales; and to the thousands of visitors who come along each year.

I have great pleasure in introducing these *Tales of South Wales*. My congratulations to Ken Radford for a fine book. And a special commendation to the schoolchildren who helped gather the stories and drew all the delightful illustrations.

Wynford Vaughan-Thomas

Preface

Tales of rogues, wrecks and rescue, of ghosts and witches, Canwyll Corph (Corpse Candles), phantom funerals and Tylwyth Teg (Fairy Folk). These, and others, have been gathered from the four counties of South Wales: from the quiet of the Black Mountains, the mining valleys of Glamorgan, farmsteads on the slopes of Mynydd Preseli and the moorlands around Cardigan Bay. Here in the land of Arthur, legendary king of the Britons, Merlin the wizard and Dylan the poet, strange tales abound, and our collection might have filled another volume.

Many of the stories have been gathered by schoolchildren who listened to tales their grandparents heard from their forbears. Where this is so, the shape of their tales and the incident which captured the children's interest are retained, and the tales unfold as they were originally written. All the illustrations have been drawn by children and students whose ages range from eight to 18.

The stories reflect the customs and superstitions of a century or more ago, and a way of life now long gone. They fall into three main categories.

(i) Where we have related accounts of historical incident every effort has been made to verify the facts, with diaries and faded newspaper cuttings.

(ii) Some are traditional legends which often have some foundation in fact. In diverse form these have been told and retold over the years. Where several accounts of one legend have been gathered we have presented those parts of the narrative which are common to them all, and sometimes we have explored little known versions.

(iii) Other tales, having no known historical foundation have been rescued from that wealth of folklore which once passed

ix

from one generation to another around the fire of a winter's evening, for it seemed a shame that they should be forgotten forever.

And so it is that this collection of stories, gathered from the hills, the valleys and the shores; from villages between the Wye Valley and St Bride's Bay, is presented for your enjoyment.

Ken Radford, March 1979

Acknowledgements

Our thanks are due primarily to the many old folk of Dyfed, Powys, Gwent and Glamorgan who have so willingly searched through their memories to recall tales told them by their forbears: tales which might otherwise be forgotten. We would also thank the schoolchildren and students of South Wales who have helped to gather these stories and have drawn all the illustrations.

More particularly our thanks are due to Ruth Exell and Kay Austin, two young ladies from the Swansea Valley, for the bizzare tales they have collected from the little known villages; Mr Wynne Davies N.D.D., A.T.D., the Art Tutor at Swansea's Teacher Training College and Mrs J.H. Perry, Art Teacher at Mynyddbach Comprehensive School, Swansea, who have been responsible for selecting and compiling the illustrations; Mr John Roberts B.A., whose translations have been invaluable; Mr Glyn Davies B.Sc., Head of Department at Penlan Comprehensive School, Swansea, for his advice on topics relating to the Geography and the Geology of the area; and Mr J. Mansel Thomas (who sadly did not live to see this book in print) for sharing his intimate knowledge of the Gower Peninsula's history and folklore with the children of Terrace Road School.

Our thanks are also due to Grwp ap Dafydd of Cardiff for extracts from Ken Llewellyn's book *Disaster at Tynewydd*; to Gomer Press, Llandysul, for extracts from Carl Smith's *The Men of the Mumbles Head*; to Mr Gareth Williams of the Swansea Reference Library, for his patient and valued help with research.

In conclusion we would acknowledge the help of Mr H.W.R. Douglas, a grand old gentleman now in his 95th year, who wrote poems and stories of Wales long before we were born, and who remembers tales his grandfather told of strange happenings early in the 19th century.

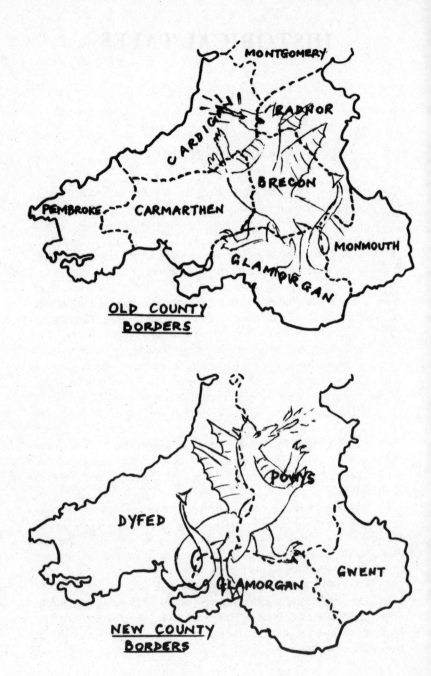

OLD COUNTY
BORDERS

NEW COUNTY
BORDERS

HISTORICAL TALES

Relics of the Past

ARTHUR'S STONE

Arthur's Stone stands on the skyline at the highest ridge of Cefn Bryn, a range of hills which form the back-bone of Gower. From its vantage point it commands a view of the whole peninsula, the Loughor estuary and, on a clear day, Lundy Island and the north coast of Devon. No-one knows how long it has stood there, but some believe it to be a neolithic burial chamber raised over a grave more than 4,000 years ago. The whole structure is thought to have once been covered with an earthen mound which has long since vanished. But there is no evidence of human remains ever having been found there.

The stone itself is a conglomerate weighing approximately 25 tons and measuring 14 feet long, eight feet high and seven feet wide. It rests on several smaller stones about two feet from the ground and was described by one child as 'like a chariot abandoned on the

hilltop'. Another saw it as 'a petrified creature crouching in the bracken ready to pounce on its prey'. Close beside it lies a rock of one-third its size which, from its shape and proportion, appears to have been sliced off the main capstone. Legend offers many explanations for the severance of the attendant fragment, confirmed by historical records to have occurred before the end of the 17th century. It is said that the stone was struck by a bolt of lightning; that it was split by a miller in search of a millstone. Earlier legend has it that the Druids of Iron Age Britain used the stone as an altar for human sacrifice.* Then, in the 6th century, St David, fearing a revival of druidic cult and worship in Wales, invoked the anger of God upon it. Before an assembled crowd he struck the capstone with his staff, breaking it in two.

The origin of the stone goes back to the Dark Ages, sometime before the year 1000 AD. According to legend, King Arthur was on his way to battle at Camlan across the Welsh border. As he passed by Craig-y-Dinas (Rock of the Fort) near Pontneddfechan in the Neath Valley, he was troubled by a piece of stone lodged in his boot. He removed the pebble and flung it as far away as he could. It came to rest on Cefn Bryn, where it grew to enormous proportions. An incredible story even as legends go, yet it bears some element of truth, for the composition of the rock in Arthur's Stone, while similar to that on Cefn Bryn, is identical in mineral constituency to the rock found in the Neath Valley. Some powerful force was needed to transport it a distance of seven miles. Geologists claim that it was the result of glacier movement during the Ice Age, perhaps 20,000 years ago.

Until the end of the last century Arthur's Stone featured in a romantic superstition. Whenever the moon was full it was customary for local girls to test the fidelity of their lovers. Each girl in turn placed on the capstone a homemade cake of barley-meal and honey. Then, ceremoniously, she danced three times around the rock structure. If her lover was faithful he would appear there in the moonlight. Otherwise it meant that he was a philanderer with no intention of making her his wife.

---

* Flecks of red sandstone embedded in the rock and assimilating bloodstains may well have led to the belief that the structure was once used as a sacrificial altar.

A few miles to the east of Cefn Bryn lies the Green Cwm, a verdant valley running north from Parkmill to Llethryd and described as the graveyard of cultures long forgotten.

Evidence of man's first occupation of the valley – a flint blade of Creswellian type – was unearthed at Cathole, a cave located in a limestone crag on the eastern side of the valley. It is a relic of some 14,000 years ago when these Palaeolithic people dwelt in the Creswell Crags of Derbyshire and the caves of Wales and Devon. Further exploration of the cave has revealed remains of the woolly rhinoceros, the mammoth, the red deer, sheep, bronze axeheads and portions of human skeletons – a chronology from the age of glacial rigour through the warmer era when the valley was completely forested. Today only spiders and bats inhabit Cathole.

In the spring of 1869 workmen making a road through the Green Cwm were removing stones from a heap on the valley bottom. After a while they came upon some large upright stones forming a chamber in which they saw portions of a skeleton. This led to the discovery of the tumulus known as Giant's Grave, built some 4,500 years ago by settlers from Brittany. It is a chambered gallery tomb occupying an area of 60 feet long, 50 feet wide and five feet high. The direction of the cairn is north to south, with the entrance at the south. And here the bones of human beings who died centuries ago were interred, together with their lances and knives for hunting in the after-life.

The Green Cwm, with its northern light, awful stillness and

memories of ages past, has an aura which visitors never forget. An 11-year-old girl, who visited the peninsula on a field study of Gower's natural resources, wrote of the Green Cwm:

'It was late in the afternoon when we passed through the Cwm. There was no sound of footsteps in the soft grass and shadows fell around the cairn ... The valley was very quiet and everyone spoke in whispers ... We were walking towards a cave and decided to explore it. Once we were in there an eerie feeling came over me. I felt that someone was watching from the dark corners. All the time someone was watching. We called out into the cave and voices came back from deep inside, like echoes from a long time ago.'

The Women of Mumbles Head

One morning, during the winter of 1883, a fierce storm swept across the Bristol Channel. The Prussian barque, *Admiral Prinz Adelbert*, her rudder lost, was seen drifting toward the rocks a quarter of a mile to the west of Mumbles Head. A steam-tug, *Flying Scud*, was attempting to tow her, but the stout hawser snapped like a slender thread and the barque was dashed upon the rocks. As the storm bell tolled and the tug sounded her whistle, the Mumbles lifeboat was launched, and seven of her crew and six volunteers struck out with their oars through the inner sound and into the teeth of the angry waves.

The lifeboat crew cast anchor to windward of the barque and grappling irons were thrown aboard. Two men were rescued by this means. A third man was being hauled in when a tremendous sea swept away the barque's masts and tossed the lifeboat against the side of the Prussian vessel. It lay capsized almost under the stern of the wreck. Some of the lifeboat crew were thrown into the water while some held fast to the lifelines. Several managed to swim to the shelter of the caves, but four crewmen lost their lives, stunned by the collision and drowned in the swirling water.

For a while the coxswain clung to the upturned boat, his eyes searching around for survivors, his four sons among them. Despite serious head injuries he was able to pull one of his sons out of the water and scramble ashore with him on the crest of a breaker. But

his son was already dead. Now he could do no more than call for assistance and watch, helplessly, as the rest of the crew fought for survival.

His cries were heard by the lighthouse keeper, the keeper's two daughters and a soldier belonging to the battery. They went forward where two crewmen near exhaustion were being driven nearer the rocks. Ignoring their father's warning, the women ventured farther, wading out almost beyond their depth into the icy water. In his report of the rescue the injured coxswain tells how the women knotted their shawls together and repeatedly hurled the improvised lifeline toward the drowning men. Clement Scott's narrative poem* which, in the latter years of the 19th century was learned and recited by schoolchildren, describes the incident more melodramatically:

>...There by the rocks on the breakers,
>   These sisters hand in hand
>Beheld once more the desperate men
>   Who struggled to reach the land ...
>
>Off went the women's shawls,
>   In a second they're torn and rent,
>Then knotting them into a rope of love
>   Straight into the sea they went ...

It is now recorded in the Archives at Swansea how the heroism of the lighthouse keeper's daughters saved the lives of two men from the crew of the Mumbles Lifeboat. The tragic irony of this rescue attempt is that the barque dried at low water and the rest of her crew were able to scramble from the wreck over the rocks to the safety of the lighthouse. Had the lifeboat not put to sea no-one would have been lost. But it was a black day in the history of the Gower coast, for before dawn two steamers with all hands had been lost in Porteynon Bay.

In a Roll of Honour the following members of the Mumbles Lifeboat and Lighthouse are remembered for their gallant service while answering a call of distress from the *Admiral Prinz Adelbert* on the 27th day of January, 1883. A memorial plaque and stained glass window can be seen today at All Saint's, the parish church of Oystermouth.

* A poem to commemorate the incident was written by Clement Scott (1841-1904). This stirring but factually inaccurate poem earned considerable acclaim at the end of the 19th century. Much of its narrative is contradicted in official accounts of the tragedy.

Drowned at Sea:
John Jenkins (2nd coxswain) aged 37, who left a widow and six children
William Jenkins, aged 35, who left a widow and two children (both sons of the coxswain)
William Macnamara (son-in-law of the coxswain) aged 40, who left a widow and four children, including one-month-old twins
William Rogers, aged 36, who left a widow and seven children
Also drowned: the carpenter of Admiral Prinz Adelbert

Injured:
Jenkin Jenkins (coxswain)
Jenkin Jenkins Jnr., George Jenkins (also sons of the coxswain)

Rescued:
William Rosser, John Thomas

Rescuers:
Abraham Ace (lighthouse keeper)
Jessie Ace and Margaret Wright (daughters of lighthouse keeper)
Artilleryman Edward Hutchings

The Rescuers

Toward the end of the last century maritime activity in the Bristol Channel was at its height. The Cambrian newspaper of that time reports 'upward of 200 vessels weather-bound in the Mumbles' Roads'. Each year accounts of disaster off the coast of South Wales were reported, for then, as now, merchant shipping had to overcome the hazards of rocky shores, shallows and shifting sands. Statistics show that during the period 1830-1858 156 vessels were wrecked between Oxwich Point and Swansea Bay, with the loss of more than 400 lives. It was not until the R.N.L.I. took over the Swansea station in 1863 that a rescue service was organised. Three years later the lifeboat was moved to the village of Mumbles and was manned by a crew of volunteers who lived there.

During the past 100 years or more, from the days when the lifeboat was pulled with oars and driven by sail to the more sophisticated craft of today, countless lives have been saved by these gallant rescuers. But such service is not rendered without loss of life and serious injury.

Here are two stories of their courage and sacrifice.

January 31, 1903:

It was on this Saturday afternoon that the Irish steamer, *Christina*, making for Port Talbot for the purpose of taking on a cargo of coal, went aground near the entrance to the harbour. The decision was made by the ship's captain and the harbour master to await high tide when an attempt would be made to refloat the vessel. Although the steamer was in no immediate danger the lifeboat, with 14 hands aboard, set out under sail the following afternoon to render any assistance which might be necessary.

The sea was calm when the ill-fated boat left Mumbles, but as she neared the stranded *Christina* the wind freshened and the coxswain decided to seek shelter in the harbour. On nearing the bar she was struck by a heavy sea and the helmsman lost control of the steering. The boat filled with water and then capsized as a further sea crashed upon her. She righted herself almost at once, and five of the crewmen managed to recover their positions in the boat. But it was then that six members of the lifeboat, *James Stephenson*, met with their deaths, for they were dashed against the walls of the breakwater and eventually drowned, despite gallant efforts to save them by the harbour master, shore workers and three French sailors.

Meanwhile the other eight crewmen struggled to survive in the fearful sea. Eye witnesses describe how 'three survivors jumped from the boat and with superhuman effort swam clear of the boulders to reach the safety of a sandy beach beside the north pier'; and of how 'the bowman fought relentlessly among the towering waves to rescue three of his comrades before he became exhausted and was hauled to the shore by a French seaman'.

When darkness came all hope was abandoned. The loss of six crewmen came 20 years, almost to the day, after the tragedy of the *Admiral Prinz Adelbert* rescue,* bringing more grief to the villagers of Mumbles.

The hardship suffered by the families of the crewmen – mainly

---

* See the Women of Mumbles Head.

fishermen – can be imagined when one considers the dependants they left behind:

Tom Rogers (coxswain) aged 40 – seven children.
Daniel Claypitt (2nd coxswain) aged 36 – 13 children.
George Michael, aged 45 – nine children.
David John Morgan (a survivor of the 1883 disaster) aged 50 – seven children.
David Gammon – two children.
Robert Smith, aged 40 – unmarried.

April 23, 1947:

Perhaps the worst sea disaster in the stormy history of the South Wales coast occurred little more than 30 years ago, when volunteers of the Mumbles lifeboat put to sea in atrocious conditions in answer to a call of distress.

At 7 o'clock that night the 7,000 ton steamer, *Samtampa*, bound for Newport, was dashed on the rocks at Sker Point about 300 yards off shore. The ship was broken in two by the force of the impact and her crew huddled together helplessly on the bridge on one half of the wreck, for the sea was too rough to launch the ship's lifeboat. In the gale-lashed waves the other half split again, throwing debris and thousands of gallons of crude oil into the sea. A life-saving crew at Porthcawl made repeated attempts to fire rocket lines aboard, but they were all held in the force of the gale and fell short.

As the light faded, nothing more was seen of the *Samtampa*'s crew until some of their bodies were washed ashore, lit up in the water by the headlights of cars which had been focussed on the broken vessel. When the tide had receded police and rescue squads were able to wade out to her. But with only torchlights to guide them they were unable to venture far into the wreck. There were no signs of life aboard and it was feared that many of the crew had been caught amidships and buried in the debris. The search continued at day break. Later that morning four bodies, all blackened with oil, were recovered from the seashore and laid on the sand dunes. None of the *Samtampa*'s 40 crew survived.

It was shortly before 6 o'clock the previous evening, while the steamer was drifting toward Nash Shoal, when the maroons were fired and the lifeboat put out in a 70 mph gale toward the open channel and breasting the heavy sea. With a visibility of five miles she was seen from the pier to be having difficulty. After searching for more than an hour and failing to locate the steamer, she returned to

Mumbles. The crew was given further direction on the position of the *Samtampa* and later put to sea again in a renewed effort to rescue the distressed crew. In a little while she was out of sight.

There was no news of the lifeboat throughout the night. Early the next morning a report was received from the Porthcawl Police that the upturned lifeboat, with no sign of its crew, had been found washed up in the region of Sker Point, caught fast in a belt of jagged rocks 500 yards to the east of the wrecked steamer.

All eight members of the lifeboat crew perished in the rescue attempt. They were: William J. Gammon (coxswain) holder of the R.N.L.I.'s gold medal and winner of the lifeboatman's V.C.; William Noel (2nd coxswain); Gilbert Davies, mechanic; Ernest Griffin, second mechanic; William Thomas, bowman; Richard Smith; Ronald Thomas and William Howell. Their graves lie side by side at Oystermouth Cemetery.

There is an unusual postscript to the story of the 1947 disaster. It is said that for some time before the fateful day, the wife of one of the crewmen was troubled by a strange recurring dream in which she saw a coffin being carried past the lifeboat cottage, and crowds of people standing silently at the roadside.

An interesting book entitled *The Men of Mumbles Head* (Gomer Press, Llandysul) traces the history of the lifeboat station from its founding to the present day. The book was written by Carl Smith, a present member of the lifeboat crew and a descendant of lifeboatmen drowned in all three Mumbles lifeboat disasters.

The Tynewydd Disaster

The Rhondda Valley in the 19th century has been described as 'a wild and mountainous region where nature seemed to reign in stern and unbroken silence'. And there, where the Rhondda Fach and the Rhondda Fawr combine and flow into the River Taff, was the shaft that led down to the Tynewydd pit. This was the scene of disaster and dramatic rescue which lasted for 10 days in the year 1877.

It was just before 4 p.m. on the 11th day of April. Below the ground, men, boys and ponies were working in the dark, rocky passages. Sweaty, black faces and white teeth caught the glimmer of light from the lamps placed low at each end of the coal face. Their shift almost over, the colliers prepared to leave the pit. They could be raised to the surface only in small parties, so by 4 p.m. 14 men were still at their place of work.

Thomas Morgan turned to his sons, William and Richard.

'Time to go home, boys.'

They put on their jackets, collected their food tins, tools and water bottles and moved away from the face down the slope to the bottom-level-heading.* There they turned right and made their way toward the Gelynog Dip which led up to the shaft and eventually to the cage which would lift them to daylight and the sweet mountain air. Passing a stall door where other men were still working, Thomas beat a friendly 'goodnight' on the stout timber with his mandrill.

They had gone only a short distance when they were stopped by a rush of air toward them. A low, rumbling sound was followed by a roar, and a sudden torrent of water, two feet deep, threatened to sweep them away. Thomas cried out to his sons as they stumbled along. But his voice was lost in the rush of wind. The flood swept by, dislodging rocks and timber props.

They moved back the way they had come. On their left a cross-heading* branched off. They turned into it, because any turning left must take them up the slope of the seam. Scrambling upward, they heard the flood as it tore by below them. As they passed through the middle level-heading* they met Edward Williams and William

* The main level-headings, or roadways, were driven in coal, and cross-headings followed the rise of the seam, that is, uphill.

12

Cassia who had just left their stall.

'Water has broken in!' Thomas shouted above the roar.

Together, the five men continued up the cross-heading toward a windway which ran parallel to but beneath the upper level heading. Behind them the water still raced through the workings, searching out every opening and filling it to the roof. When they reached the windway they turned left, for they knew that it connected with the Gelynog Dip. As they neared the Dip the narrow windway sloped downwards again. Each man struggled with his own fears as they approached the path to freedom. But the flood water had risen swiftly up the slope and was there before them. Their exit to safety was barred!

Morgan and Williams stood together for a moment. They were both familiar with the geography of the pit and their knowledge might yet save them. They were forced to retrace their steps, going now away from the flooding Dip, back along the low, narrow passage. They passed the place where they had entered the windway from the cross-heading and carried on to a point where the passage rose a little.

With the water level creeping up behind them, they came at last

to the highest point where the passage formed a 'hump' and then began its downward gradient. Here they were trapped, with water behind them and ahead. They felt a pressure in their ears in the pocket of compressed air. Meanwhile, the water still roared into the empty spaces below and crept up the dark walls on both sides of them. Subsequently it was learned that this 'hump' in the windway was left above the highest point reached by the flood.

Thomas Morgan beat upon the rock with a heavy stone as a signal to anyone still alive. And there, in their murky tomb, five Welsh miners, fearing their end was near, began to sing in their native language.

In their underground prison they huddled together, trapped in a pocket of compressed air. In the candle-light they saw the flood water creep up the slope on each side of them. There was nothing they could do but wait, and pray. Then, after a time, the sound of rushing water abated and they noticed that the flood level was no longer rising. With new hope they were stirred to action. Somewhere above them was the main upper-level roadway, and they knew that all roadways and windways were cut in the coal. So they took up their mandrills and began to dig upward into the seam.

The wailing alarm signal had brought a crowd of people to the pit head. Colliers on their way home to the nearby cottages came hurrying along the streets. A roll-call was then organised and it was discovered that 14 men were missing. Every miner present volunteered to help start the rescue operation.

At the bottom of the shaft the first party of rescuers found the main level heading clear of water. They heard the distant rumble of timber, rocks and empty trams carried along in the flooded caverns below. After every 10 or 20 paces forward they stopped to listen, to call out, to signal with their hammers. Then, after travelling a distance of half a mile along the roadway, the steady thud of a pick cutting into the coal seam reached their ears.

They moved toward the sound, and soon they were signalling to the entombed men through the coal barrier. The rescue team, who knew the pit well, realised that the men were trapped in the windway 30 feet below the main roadway. Before long, experienced mining engineers were helping with the rescue operation.

It was early the following morning before the barrier of coal was reduced to a thin wall. Two rescuers at a time worked side by side, digging a tunnel six feet wide down toward the windway. Other rescuers cleared the debris behind them. Now the rescue team and the trapped men were able to shout to each other through the barrier.

An engineer warned the men to stand well clear, fearing they

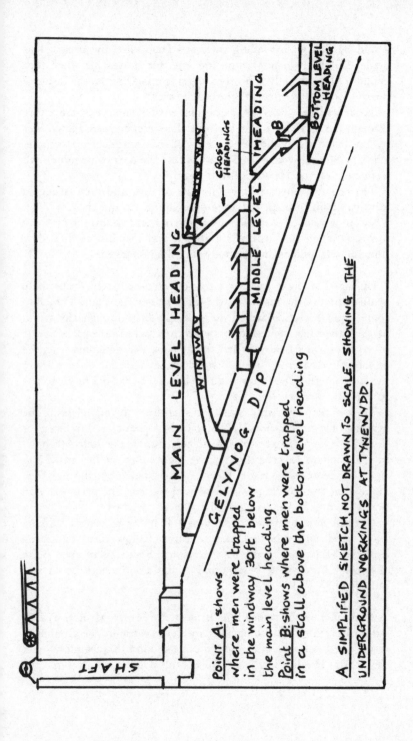

SHAFT

MAIN LEVEL HEADING

ROADWAY

WINDWAY

GELYNOG DIP

CROSS HEADINGS

MIDDLE LEVEL HEADING

BOTTOM LEVEL HEADING

A

B

Point A: shows where men were trapped in the windway 30ft below the main level heading.

Point B: shows where men were trapped in a stall above the bottom level heading

A SIMPLIFIED SKETCH, NOT DRAWN TO SCALE, SHOWING THE UNDERGROUND WORKINGS AT TYNEWYDD.

would be injured by falling rock and coal when the breach was made. But his warning came too late, for it was just then that William Morgan and his brother, digging upward from the inside of the windway, broke through the coal barrier.

Suddenly there was an explosion as the compressed air tore through the small breach in the wall. The rescuers were blown over by the blast which showered pieces of rock and coal upon them. William Morgan was hurled forward into the narrow opening with tremendous force. He was killed instantly.

The rescuers retreated for a minute or two, and then struggled forward again through the force of escaping air and choking dust. They cut a number of small holes in the barrier to allow the pressure to drop. When the rush of air abated and the dust settled, they brought out four men and the body of William Morgan.

During that night another party of rescuers fought desperately against time in the main level-heading nearer the shaft. They had come upon a section where air was escaping through the strata beneath their feet, forced up between the cracks in the rocks by the pressure of water below. When signals were heard coming from the underground caverns, they realised that they were somewhere above the stall where Edward o'r Maindy and a 13-year-old boy, Robert Rogers, had been cutting coal.

They worked feverishly, sinking a shaft from the main level to the heading below. Occasionally they paused to signal and to listen for the distant tapping to return like an echo from the prisoners trapped in the flooding caverns. But as the night wore on the answering signals were heard no more. When, at last, they broke through they found that the heading was filled with water. The prisoners had been overcome by the rising flood and were drowned.

The rescuers knew that the bodies could not be recovered until the water level had subsided and the stalls below them had been explored. But now time was precious. Seven more men were entombed somewhere below, and so far their whereabouts was unknown.

At the Tynewydd pithead the Inspector of Mines, Mr R.E. Wales, with other experienced officials, considered carefully the attempt to rescue the seven men still trapped underground. An examination of the nearby Hinde's pit, now disused and flooded, showed that the water level there had fallen by almost 100 feet, so the source of the flood at Tynewydd was known. Without delay, a large pump was installed at the bottom of the Tynewydd shaft and pipes were laid to the surface. The Gelynog Dip had now completely filled with water.

The rescue team explored the upper level-heading. They moved slowly, listening, signalling. Then, late in the afternoon, their eyes lit up with excitement when faintly, through solid rock and coal, they heard a distant tapping from the caverns below. The trapped men were located about half a mile from the shaft. New hope stirred among the crowd at the pithead when the news was relayed to them.

This illustration explains why the trapped miners saw the flood water approaching them from in front and behind. Air pressure built up in the 'hump' – the highest point in the windway.

Here is a side view of the rescue operation. Rescuers dug a tunnel down through the coal seam, from the main level heading to the windway, leaving a thin barrier wall between the rescuers and the trapped men.

When an additional pump was brought into action, 13,000 gallons of water every hour were being moved. But expert examination of plans marking the underground layout showed that pumping alone was futile. Before the immense volume of water could be removed, the men would die of exposure and starvation. Inspector Wales decided to attempt a different ploy to reach the imprisoned men.

By the early hours of April 14th, two divers, summoned from London and conveyed by special train, arrived at Tynewydd. Their task was fraught with danger; to descend through hundreds of feet of murky water, through narrow passages blocked with trams, floating timber and rubble.

17

The two divers, Davis and Purvis, began their tortuous journey. Slowly unwinding air pipes and a rope to guide them on their return to the surface, they slid down the slope of Gelynog Dip. On the Saturday afternoon, as William Morgan's funeral procession passed down the valley toward Llanwynno Church, the courageous divers made their way along black tunnels hundreds of feet below the valley floor.

They were still a long way from the trapped men when their venture proved too formidable. Surging water threw them against the roofs and walls of the caverns. Deafened by the impact with the rocks, and fearing their helmets would crack, they were forced to return to the surface.

Disappointment swept through the crowd at the pithead, but the rescuers continued with renewed determination. Their first priority was to reduce the level of the water. Pumps were set to work again, and slowly the flood was receding. By Sunday afternoon it had fallen to the level of the middle heading since pumping was now going on by every available means, at Tynewydd and at the source of the flood – the abandoned Hinde's pit a quarter of a mile away. Before long the rescue team would be able to make its final assault on the 120 feet barrier which separated them from the trapped men.

When Thomas Morgan and his sons left their work place on the previous Wednesday, they had signalled a cheery 'goodnight' to the party of men working in a nearby stall. The roar and pressure in their ears brought these men out of their stall and they were forced to retreat in the direction of the water flow, away from the bottom of Gelynog Dip. They turned left into the first cross-heading up the seam. It was Thomas Morgan's stall, 40 yards up from the bottom level-heading. Here they turned and watched the water approach them. There was no way out. There was no escape for the air either, and they felt the pressure increase as the air compressed.

And there they had been entombed for days. Like the party rescued from the windway, they too had been saved from drowning by a pocket of compressed air in the confines of the stall in which they had sought refuge. The pressure held the flood waters at bay. They had only candle-light to comfort them, and to conserve their body heat they huddled together in a tram containing a bed of small coal.

The hours passed slowly as these five despairing miners signalled and listened and prayed. They were: David Jenkins aged 40, Moses Powell aged 31, George Jenkins aged 30, Jonathan Thomas aged 25, and David Hughes, a boy of 14.

In their underground prison, day was no different from night. They were cold and hungry, and they drank the filthy water to quench their thirst. Two of them had earlier attempted to swim under water to safety, but their attempt was doomed to failure.

By Monday, April 16th, the water level was falling at an ever-increasing rate. The rescue party selected for the final desperate attempt to reach the trapped men were warned of the dangers confronting them.

That afternoon the first team, under the direction of Inspector Wales, began tunnelling down through the coal seam. Progress was slow and arduous. After four hours the six feet wide tunnel descended to a depth of only five yards.

Throughout the day and night people remained anxiously at the pithead — relatives and ordinary folk from the valleys, colliery officials and reserve rescue teams, newspaper reporters. Doctors and nurses were standing by. Everyone's thoughts and prayers were for the men buried underground.

In her cottage near the pit, Martha Hughes also prayed. Five days ago her husband and two sons had left home, perhaps never to return. She had no way of knowing that her younger son, David, was trapped in a stall with four companions; nor did she know then that her husband and her older son, Willie John, were to perish in another cavern half a mile away from David.

Now she sat alone beside an open door, knowing that she might be alone for the rest of her days.

By 4 o'clock the following afternoon the tunnel had gone almost half way down the seam. A dam was built to exclude water from the entrance to the tunnel. But although the flood was steadily falling, it was estimated that the rescue parties were now burrowing six feet below water level. A locomotive was brought up the valley and was linked by pipes to another pump placed on the main heading.

The pumping and digging continued. Meanwhile, Inspector Wales and his team of engineers considered a very difficult problem. How could they break into a chamber under pressure without killing the men as William Morgan had been killed? It was decided to build airtight doors across the tunnel, and to use a compressor inside the airlock to equalise the pressure on either side of the barrier.

From time to time signals were exchanged with the trapped men. Then, at 7 o'clock the following evening, the rescuers were near enough to shout to them through the seam. Only five men were imprisoned there. Two others, who had been working in another stall, were unaccounted for.

A considerable head of water above the stall in which the men were confined added to the danger. Events that followed brought frustration and disappointment. An unsuccessful attempt was made to pass food through holes bored in the dividing wall, and the holes were plugged. The experiment to build up pressure in the sealed-off section of the tunnel failed. To add to their peril, an escape of gas extinguished the safety lamps.

When at last the pocket of gas dispersed, there came the final and most perilous stage of the rescue. Inspector Wales decided they had only one course of action. It was a gamble, with the lives of the rescuers and the imprisoned men at stake.

Five courageous volunteers descended into the tunnel. Hoarse voices called to them faintly through the dividing wall. The prisoners were now clinging desperately to their fading hopes of survival. The holes drilled earlier through the barrier were unplugged and enlarged. At once a fearful rumble, like continuous thunder, escaped into the tunnel, with an attendant threat of gas and a danger that the roof would collapse. As the pressure was released, the water level began to rise inside the stall. An agony of suspense passed as the air escaped and the water rose.

Even when the noise abated, the presence of gas was indicated by the flaring of the safety lamps. The rescue party attacked the remaining few feet of the barrier with renewed vigour. Mercifully, the water ceased to rise when it was within inches of drowning the trapped miners.

It was mid-day on Friday, 20th April, when the last of the survivors emerged from the filth and darkness of their tomb. Some wept. Others rambled deliriously. The boy, David Hughes, asked only for news of his father and brother who, sadly, were presumed drowned in the black water a half mile away.

Shouting and singing echoed around the hillsides when the survivors and their gallant rescuers appeared in the sunlight at the pithead. There have been many disasters in the Welsh coalfields over the years, with greater suffering and loss of life. But the flooding of Tynewydd will be remembered for its 10 days of suspense and for the courage and ingenuity of the rescuers.

Following the Tynewydd disaster there came an announcement from Queen Victoria:

> The Albert Medal, hitherto bestowed only for gallantry in saving life at sea, shall be extended to similar actions on land, and the first medals struck for this purpose shall be conferred on the heroic rescuers of the Welsh miners.

The London Gazette of August 7th, 1877, published the names of the 24 men on whom this honour was bestowed.

Twm Shôn Catti

Lonely hills, shadowy woodland, mountain streams edged with craggy rocks. This was the wild countryside near the border between Carmarthen and Cardigan where Twm Shôn Catti spent his life.

More than 400 years ago in the village of Tregaron a son was born to a girl called Catherine Jones. The child was given the names Thomas John. He had no surname for he was born out of wedlock.* So he was known as Catherine's Thomas John, which, in his native language, is Twm Shôn Catti. And when he grew to manhood there was no greater loved rascal in the whole of Wales for, although ostensibly a yeoman farmer, he chose the ways of a rogue and outlaw. To this day tales of his escapades are told in the taverns of Carmarthen and Cardigan where, affectionately, he is remembered as the Robin Hood of Wales, for he never stole a bag of gold from a rich man without sharing it among the poor.

Midway through the 16th century the life of a peasant was hard, and social injustice kindled much bitterness. Folk scratched a living from the land or worked as lead miners, seeking wealth in the bowels of the earth. Thieves were hanged, and their bodies left on the gibbet as a deterrent to others. Folk were pinioned in the stocks for not doffing their caps to the vicar. And in these times of poverty and persecution Twm Shôn gave courage and pride of heritage to the common folk of the county. He engaged in every kind of roguery from highway robbery to cattle stealing. Although he had the strength of a lion he was better known for his cunning and audacity than as a man of violence. But despite his mischievous ways he was proud of his noble blood, and vowed that one day he would be respected in all the land.

For all his misdeeds Twm Shôn was never identified or captured by the Sheriff's men, for as a highwayman he usually wore the mask of a hawk, and while he practised his skullduggery in the towns and villages he was a master of disguise of voice and appearance.

* It is generally believed that the father of Catherine's child was Sir John Wynn of the noble family of Gwydir in the north.

One day, as he wandered through Tregaron, he came upon a wealthy merchant who strode arrogantly along the cobbled street, leading his fine grey stallion. A ragged boy stepped in his path, begging a penny for a loaf of bread. Angrily, the merchant brushed him aside, striking the boy with his crop. Farther along the street Twm Shôn saw the horse tethered beside a tavern, while inside the merchant took a drink or two of ale. In a little while the fine grey was galloping over the hills with Twm Shôn in the saddle.

The merchant was furious when he discovered his loss. But, search though he may, his horse was nowhere to be found. Presently a simple farmer came riding into the village. His horse had a short cropped mane, its flanks and forelegs speckled black.

'Beg your pardon, sir,' he said, doffing his cap when the merchant questioned him. 'No, sir. There's nobody I've seen hereabouts riding a grey stallion. And likely you'll never see him again,' he added as the merchant eyed his speckled mount. The farmer slapped his horse on the rump. 'I shouldn't be sorry if some thief stole this miserable beast. Has a real stubborn streak in him and travels no faster than a cart horse. I'd gladly sell him for five sovereigns.'

The merchant studied the stallion's sturdy limbs and fine coat, and then thought of his weary journey home on foot. 'I'll give you two,' he said, taking advantage of the guileless farmer.

And so a bargain was struck. The merchant rode off over the hills on the speckled horse with short cropped mane. When he had gone out of sight, the farmer discarded his brimmed hat and rumpled coat. And it was Twm Shôn Catti who stood there smiling to himself, for he knew that in a while, when the mane grew long again and the painted speckles faded away, the merchant would recognise his fine grey stallion.

To the beggar-boy in the street he tossed a golden sovereign. The other he spent with his friends in the tavern, drinking ale and singing old Welsh songs.

On another occasion Twm Shôn had stolen a prize bull from one of the wealthiest farmers in the district and had given it to a poor farmer from Llangeitho who had fallen on hard times. No-one had set eyes on the thief, but the audacity of the deed had aroused the farmer's suspicion. With a pistol tucked in his belt he rode off to the home of Catti Jones, and as he approached the house an old man shuffled by.

'I'm looking for Twm Shôn Catti,' the visitor said with a scowl. 'Whereabouts will I find him?'

The old man chuckled. 'This is where he lives,' he explained in a hoarse whisper. 'But when you knock on the front door he'll escape round the back.'

So while the angry farmer strode around the back the old man was left to hold the horse's reins and whip. But when the farmer returned his horse was gone, for as he was searching for Twm Shôn Catti, it was Twm Shôn himself who threw off the ragged clothes of an old man and galloped across the fields to the farmer's house. There he dismounted, hammered on the door and delivered his message to the startled lady of the house.

'Pardon me, ma'am. Your husband has sent me on an urgent errand from the market in Tregaron where he is bidding for a new prize bull. I am to hurry back with 30 sovereigns from his chest. You can see that he has trusted me with his fine horse and silver-handled whip.'

The messenger had a pleasant smile and frank blue eyes, so the lady did as he asked. But Twm Shôn did not return to Tregaron with the farmer's golden coins. Instead he journeyed through many a village, sharing his small fortune with the peasant folk he met on the highways and in the taverns.

It was an adventure on the highway that put an end to Twm Shôn's lawless escapades. One day he stopped a coach on the road from Llandovery to Llanwrtyd Wells. Looking down the muzzle of his pistol was the powerful squire of Llandovery, who was invited to hand over all his money and valuables.

'You see, my lord,' explained Twm Shôn, who was wearing his favourite disguise, 'the hawk is a bird of prey and here among the Welsh hills you are just another sparrow.'

Beside the squire sat his beautiful daughter with whom Twm Shôn fell in love at first sight. He left the rings on her fingers and a necklace about her throat, 'Although,' he said, 'they can never match the sparkle in your eyes.'

The squire's daughter was secretly attracted to Twm Shôn's sonorous voice and charming manner. But not so the squire, for the moment he returned to Llandovery he raised all the forces of the law against the highwayman, who was then forced to flee for his life. But, because of his love for the squire's daughter, he never strayed far. He found refuge in a cave among the rocks where the Tywi River comes out of the mountains. From there he braved capture to visit the squire's hall in Llandovery, assuming one or another of his many disguises. Time and again he risked his life for a glance at the lady he loved or a moment or two in her company. Persistently he begged her to marry him, and at length she learned to admire his courage and loved him in return.

According to the story, they were married secretly in a little church on the hillside. That was the end of Twm Shôn's days as an outlaw. With his wife's help, and her father's influence, he was pardoned for all his wrong-doing and lived to become a poet and a justice of the peace, a commission which he held until the end of his life.

If ever you pass by the place where the valleys of the Camddwr and the Tywi meet, follow the path close to the river as it climbs up beside a steep gorge. There you will come to Twm Shôn Catti's cave – his refuge from the hangman. Today it has little attraction, and you will marvel how anyone could have lived in such a place. Above the sounds of rushing water and the sheep bleating on the hills, you may hear the haunting notes from a ram's horn, for that was how Twm Shôn Catti called to his followers.

Little Old Lady

It was the year 1895 – a time of deep depression throughout South
Wales. In the mining valleys colliers were without work, without
hope, struggling desperately to protect their families from starvation
and the cold of winter. There was no unemployment benefit in those
days, and no social services. Deprived of the dignity of earning a
living, folk had to beg, borrow or steal in order to survive. When all
else failed, families were committed to the parish workhouses,
known then as the 'poor law bastille', where men were separated
from their wives and children; where self respect was sacrificed just
for food and shelter.

Annie was now 11-years-old. Already family responsibilities
weighed heavily on her shoulders, for with Ellen dead and gone she
was now the oldest child. There were six brothers and sisters
younger than she; some to feed and rock to sleep and some to keep
from mischief, while her father and mother worked by day and night

earning shillings and pennies to buy food and pay the rent for their small terraced house.

Annie's father could no longer work on the coal face, for since 'the dust' had affected his lungs he hadn't the stamina to wield a pick and shovel. So he was thankful to accept the job of tending the pit ponies during the night shift. His wages were poor, but there were many other men with none at all. Often he took his terrier, Cymro, underground with him. The dog was a remarkable rat catcher, and since a penny was paid for every rat's tail brought to the surface (a measure to reduce the menace of vermin underground), there were times when Cymro earned more money than his master during an eight-hour shift.

Early in the morning, as Annie's father came over the hillside on his way home from work, Annie and her mother rose from their beds. They lit the kitchen fire and prepared breakfast for the family. Their food was plain, and often not enough to stave off the pangs of hunger. Usually meals consisted of bread and beef dripping or hot vegetable stew, and sometimes there was offal from the butcher. The older children went to school, and at midday they were fed at the soup kitchen. But, more often than not, Annie was kept at home to help with the household chores, especially when the young ones were poorly and needed constant attention.

When breakfast was over, Father went to his bed while Annie tended to the children and Mother filled the tub with water boiled on the open fire, ready for the day's laundry. The money she earned from taking in washing helped to buy clogs for the children and a few articles of winter clothing.

Soon the kitchen was filled with steaming clothes and the rhythmic sound of the rubbing board. Annie kneeled over the tub, her back aching, strands of hair hung limply about her neck. She had the care-worn face of a little old lady; heavy-eyed from restless nights, and never a smile on her lips.

When the weather was fine the clothes were hung to dry at the foot of the hill beyond the back wall. Then the flat-irons were heated before the fire and the drudgery continued well into the afternoon.

Annie liked the summertime best for then, during the long evenings, she could sometimes play with other children or walk alone over the hills. She liked the morning sun which lit up her room. Winter was a relentless struggle against the cold. There were days when she set off with a sack slung over her shoulder to gather

up the coal which had fallen from the trams and lay beside the track near the colliery, or to forage among the slag heaps. By dusk she would return home, black and numbed, laden with fuel to stoke the fire the next day. At night her sisters would huddle beside her in bed, and sometimes a tear would shine in the candle-light.

Sadly, the winter of 1895 was Annie's last, for then her life came to an end almost before it had begun. In December she fell ill, and as the month drew on she became worse. On Christmas Eve the frost on the window panes glistened in the firelight. The family sat in the warm glow, telling stories and singing carols. As usual the children hung their stockings at the foot of the bed, but the nuts and sweets and bright new penny brought little sparkle to Annie's eyes. Her face was flushed with fever and her resistance was slipping away. With modern drugs and medical knowledge probably she would have survived, but as it was before the new year she was dead.

For three days her body lay in its little coffin, with a veil of lace spread over her face. Annie had precious little she could call her own, but now her sole possession, an old rag doll, lay in the coffin beside her. On the fourth day folk gathered at the house for the funeral. There was a service simply recited, a hymn sadly sung, and then the cortege set off on its long walk to the cemetery.

Today Annie lies in an unmarked grave on a hillside at Cymmer in the Afan Valley. Many years ago her family laid flowers there every Palm Sunday, and a wooden cross with a brief epitaph written upon it marked her resting place. It said: 'Here lies Annie Ellacott, died 29th December, 1895, aged 11. God keep her.' But the cross has long since rotted away and weeds have overgrown the mound of earth.

Home Sweet Home

Waterton Court was a fine country home standing on the outskirts of the old market town of Bridgend in the county of Glamorgan. Many years ago it was the home of Madam Adelina Patti, the well known opera singer. Although renowned throughout Europe and beyond, she never forgot her affinity with ordinary folk. This tale, recalled by an old gentleman now in his 95th year, tells of her affection for an innkeeper – a widow known to all the villagers as Kitty Abergarw.

It so happened that one summer day Adelina Patti and her husband came to the village of Brynmenyn* for the salmon fishing in the Ogmore River. At the end of the day they rested at the Miller's Arms, an old tavern standing where the Garw and the Ogmore flow together. And it was there that her friendship with the widow began.

Throughout that evening they talked at length. Madam Patti told of lands far beyond the shores of Wales, while Kitty spoke of home; of the hills and rivers and the land of song. In the months that followed, Adelina Patti and her husband came often to the Miller's Arms, and with each visit her friendship with Kitty grew. The widow admired the worldly charm of her companion, yet strangely never learned of her reputation. She never tired of the tales of foreign lands – cities of Europe and America; the shores of the Mediterranean. Although often she dreamed of far off places, Kitty's heart was in her homeland.

One evening she stood at the door of the Miller's Arms, saying farewell to Adelina. A traveller at the inn watched her wave until the carriage was out of sight. He recognised Adelina and wondered what she and the innkeeper had in common. Kitty overheard him describe her as 'Baroness Patti, the famous opera singer'.

Once she had learned of Adelina's reputation she was unusually quiet whenever they were together. There were no more homely tales; no fun and laughter. Adelina was puzzled. Then one day,

---

* Brynmenyn: the hill of butter, so named because of the wide expanse of golden gorse growing there.

when she guessed the reason for Kitty's uneasiness, she said to her, 'My voice is a gift which I share with everyone – especially my dearest friends.'

So, on that summer evening in a country tavern at Brynmenyn, the voice that had entertained the kings and princes of Europe sang for a dear friend: for Kitty Abergarw, to charm the friendship they had known. The song she chose brought tears to Kitty's eyes.

> 'Mid pleasures and palaces
> Though we may roam,
> Be it ever so humble,
> There's no place like home.

Some years later Madam Patti lived at Craig-y-Nos, a rambling 19th century house in the shadows of the Brecon Beacons and near Dan yr Ogof Caves. Today Craig-y-Nos is a home for old folk, and the private theatre which she built there is still used.

Baroness Cederstrom Adelina Patti, born in 1843, made her debut as an opera singer in New York at the age of 16. She married an Italian count and is remembered as one of the greatest coloratura sopranos of all time.

'Home, Sweet Home', the song she sang at the Miller's Arms, became her favourite. It was a special request at many of her concerts. She once said that whenever she sang these simple lyrics she thought affectionately of the yellow-tipped hills and salmon rivers of Brynmenyn, and of the warm-hearted lady she would never forget.

The Wreckers

Around the coastline of Wales there are many stretches of water dangerous to shipping. Sandy shallows, rocky reefs, swift-flowing tides and hidden currents all present a threat to seafarers. In the days of sail, with no radar or radio communication, the task of navigating near the shore was more perilous. In those days seamen relied on beacon fires and warning lights burning on the hills and cliffs to guide them through the danger.

Many stories are told of ruthless gangs who lured seamen to their doom by lighting false beacons on the shore. The ships were wrecked, cargoes were plundered and crews were murdered or left to drown.

Here are three tales of such men:

(1) Early in the 19th century on the hills above Marros Sands, which stretch along the shore of Carmarthen Bay, there stood an isolated farmhouse. It was the home of a farmer, his wife and their teenage son.

There came a time when misfortune befell them: two years of lean harvest, disease among the cattle and then, discouraged, the son left home to seek his fortune elsewhere. So the fields were neglected and the farmer and his wife became poor. Perhaps it was poverty and bitterness which led them along the path they were to follow in the years ahead.

After a while, they joined a gang of wreckers who operated along that south-eastern coast of Carmarthen. Night after night they were at work burning false lights around their farmhouse above the Telpin Sands, luring many a ship on to the treacherous shallows which shifted with the tides. And as a result of their activities the couple prospered.

One morning, while they were plundering the cargo from a wreck which had foundered in the shallows, they came upon the body of a survivor lying face down on the beach. As always the wreckers showed no mercy, for they lived by the philosophy that 'dead men tell no tales'. The farmer picked up a heavy rock and crushed the skull of the helpless seaman. Then, as they dragged the body away

to hide it in a cave, they recognised the features of their own son.

It is said that from that day there was never a light to be seen around the farmhouse on the hill, and that the farmer and his wife spent the rest of their days in bitter remorse.

(2) The little village of Penycoedcae (above the forest field) is situated on the hills to the north-east of Llanharan. The village looks down over the valley of the Ogmore in the Vale of Glamorgan.

Toward the end of the 18th century Penycoedcae was the home of one of the most notorious wreckers known around the coast of Wales. He was a local squire who lived in a grand old manor house built on the hilltop and commanding a view of the county as far as Porthcawl, a coastal town 15 miles to the south-west.

On stormy nights he lit beacon fires on the turrets of his house.

Although the coast was far away the fires burned brightly against the sky. Many a merchant ship sailing through the Bristol Channel had been lured toward the rocky shore. Along the cliff-tops at the water's edge the squire's band of wreckers kept watch. Like predators stalking their prey they made ready to seize the cargo from the wrecks and to murder the unfortunate survivors. For their deeds they were sometimes rewarded with golden coins, tobacco and kegs of brandy.

For a long time the wreckers continued to loot and kill, and the squire became rich from his plunder. Many years passed. As he grew older his thoughts dwelt more and more on the seamen he had lured to their deaths. Often he was awakened by frightful nightmares and imagined that the ghosts of his victims had returned to haunt him. It is said that his fear later turned to madness and that one night he either fell or threw himself from the high turret where once the beacon fire glowed.

Everyone agreed that the squire had received a just retribution. And even today, when storm clouds roll over the hills and the night is dark, there are folk in the village who claim that the voice of the squire can be heard crying out in terror.

(3) One of the most dangerous stretches of water around the coast of South Wales lies to the south of Carmarthenshire. Swift-flowing currents from the mouth of the Afon Tywi and the Gwendraeth swirl around Tywyn Point and the sands of Cefn Sidan. Here the waters are shallow and the reefs lie hidden beneath the surface.

Late in the 18th century wrecks were discovered from time to time lying in the shallows. Their cargoes had been looted and the crews slain. Often the bodies lay on the sand, left by the ebbing tide.

For a long while no-one could understand why so many vessels had run aground on that particular beach, for the dangerous currents lay well to the north. And the identity of the murderers remained a mystery although a careful watch was kept along the shore. Then one night, as a strong wind blew over the channel from the south-west, a beachcomber made his way home along the shore. He watched distant beacons become dim and go out. Then new fires flared on the edge of Pembrey Forest. The breakers grew tall and crashed upon the beach. Presently he saw a light glowing near the water's edge. As it drew closer he could distinguish a lantern on the foremast of a ship. A moment later the vessel foundered in the shallows. First he heard the voices of sailors calling out in alarm. Then, from out of the darkness of the forest, came a score of men rushing toward the water. He could make out their silhouettes brandishing axes and wading toward the stranded ship. There followed shouts of anger and cries of terror.

After a while the cries were heard no more. The plunderers returned to the forest with all the loot they could carry, leaving the bodies of their victims lying in the shallow water.

The wreckers along the south coast of Carmarthenshire were feared by all who sailed the Bristol Channel. Most of them escaped capture. To this day they are remembered as the Hatchetmen of Pembrey Forest. Their reign of terror lasted for many years.

Hundreds of seafaring men shipwrecked off the Welsh coast may have died unnecessarily. If they were not murdered by the wreckers they were unlikely to receive help from others, for superstitious folk in those days believed that anyone rescued from drowning was stolen from the sea. It was said that for the rest of their lives they would be plagued with misfortune and that in the end the sea would retrieve its loss, sometimes taking both lives in return.

Dic Penderyn

Early in the 19th century the mining valleys of South Wales were torn with industrial strife. There were no trade unions and workers were at the mercy of their employers. Colliers, already struggling desperately to feed and clothe their families, were given a cruel ultimatum by the colliery owners – to work longer hours for less wages or to lose their jobs and their homes and accept the cold charity of the workhouse. It was a time of poverty and bitterness.

The following is a story of an ordinary Welsh miner who is remembered to this day as a symbol of social injustice.

In 1807 at a cottage named Penderyn in the parish of Pyle a son, Richard, was born to Lewis Lewis. Nothing is known of Richard's mother, but it is known that he had an elder sister who later married a clergyman. Although the story of Richard Lewis is well known throughout the Welsh valleys, no-one will recall his name, for he is always remembered as 'Dic Penderyn'.

At the outbreak of the Merthyr Tydfil riots in 1831 he had left his native Aberavon to live in Merthyr where he worked on the coal face. Rioting began on the 2nd June with an attack on the house of the clerk to the Court of Requests. Troops were called for by the magistrates, and the next day a company of the 93rd Highland Regiment arrived. Outside a local inn they were surrounded by a crowd, among whom was Dic Penderyn. Incited by Lewis Lewis, the crowd rushed forward, seizing the soldiers' muskets in an attempt to disarm them. An ugly scene ensued. The soldiers fired into the crowd, killing and wounding a number of persons. Several soldiers were injured.

There is no evidence to suggest that Dic Penderyn took any part in this rioting, nor in the mutinous activities that followed. An ammunition party from Brecon was attacked; Swansea Yeomanry were ambushed and disarmed.

Although he protested his innocence, Dic Penderyn was arrested at Merthyr Tydfil and charged with riotously assembling and with attacking and wounding one Donald Black of the 93rd Highland Regiment. He was tried at Cardiff Assizes. Questioned by the court, the wounded soldier admitted that although he recognised the accused as one of the crowd, he did not know who had attacked him. However, two merchants, both of Merthyr, gave evidence of identification, and their testimony was largely responsible for his conviction. Dic Penderyn was condemned to death, the execution being fixed for 31st July.

A petition, endorsed by more than 10,000 signatures, was drawn up for Dic's reprieve. Then, following an appeal by a Quaker philanthropist and through the good offices of Lord Brougham, the Lord Chancellor, the Home Secretary granted a stay of execution for two weeks. When this time elapsed, no further evidence had come to light and the verdict was upheld.

At 8 o'clock on Saturday, 13th August, 1831, Dic Penderyn, aged 23, was publicly executed at Cardiff Gaol. Four Wesleyan Methodist ministers, who had been with him during his last hours, accompanied him to the scaffold. Thousands of people stood silently as the funeral procession passed through the Vale of Glamorgan on Sunday, 14th August. He was buried at St Mary's churchyard, Aberavon, but his body was not taken into the church. Outside the churchyard wall his brother-in-law, the Rev. Morgan Howells, told the crowd how an ordinary miner whose life had hardly begun had left a world of cruel injustice. It was a scene of great emotion.

It was more than 40 years later, in 1874, when a Congregational minister, the Rev. Evan Evans, reported a deathbed confession to him by a man who revealed that it was he who had wounded Donald Black of the 93rd Highland Regiment. He had remained silent while an innocent man paid for his crime.

The name of Dic Penderyn will be remembered in the Welsh mining valleys until the last black scar has disappeared from the hillsides.

House of Shadows

From Merthyr Mawr in the county of Glamorgan a quiet road leads north toward Bridgend, crossing the Ogmore river at Chapel Hill, a stretch of parkland south of the main highway. No-one who came upon such a peaceful place, with its patches of woodland and hills strewn with isolated farmhouses, would imagine that long years ago it was the scene of fearful murder. Although we are told that the horrors perpetrated in that area around Merthyr Mawr are true, over the years the story has fallen into the realms of legend.

In the middle of the 18th century the stage-coach route from the west stopped at the river. Passengers who wished to continue their journey east crossed over the ford and made their way on foot to a highway one-and-a-half miles farther south where they could board the London-bound stage at Ewenny. Beside this rough track (now a stretch of the B4265) stood an old tavern where many travellers called for food and ale, or broke their journey for a night's rest. Judged by its location it must have appeared a dismal place to anyone passing by for, built in a wooded dell, it was almost hidden from view, and its walls were cloaked in shadow.

The landlord was remembered as a violent, coarse-featured man, with red hair and fiery temper. Strange rumours about the tavern spread throughout the county. There were many occasions when travellers who had been known to spend the night there were never seen again. Whenever enquiries were made the landlord simply denied all knowledge of them. According to local tales they often drank heartily throughout the evening and then, while they lay asleep, they were robbed of their money and valuables and silently smothered under the bed clothes. By murdering them in this way the landlord and his accomplices made sure that there would be neither bloodstains to arouse the suspicion of other guests nor any marks of violence to be seen upon them. The victims were then thrown into the Ogmore and usually their bodies were washed out into the bay.

In those days there was no organised police force, so the disappearance of guests and the mysterious drownings were never investigated. But suspicion fell on the tavern and travellers stayed

away. For many years the place was almost deserted, for only rogues and outlaws went there. It became a haven for these smugglers and highwaymen. The landlord, together with his gang of mercenary followers, organised constant forays along the main road, waylaying lone travellers as they journeyed to and from Bridgend.*

Their reign of terror continued for a long time. Anyone who travelled alone on the roads south of Bridgend between the Ogmore

* During the 18th century Bridgend was the centre of the South Wales textile industry. It attracted many packmen who bought and sold their merchandise and transported it by mule to the market places.

and Ewenny rivers did so at their peril. Over the years the landlord prospered. He was never brought to task and lived well on the wealth he had plundered until he died, an old man, in 1820.

Soon after his death a main road bridge was built in Bridgend at which time the tavern outlived its purpose. Uninhabited, it fell to ruin and crumbled away.

A gruesome discovery was made in the early years of this century, when the ruined building was demolished. In a cavern beneath the cellar were found traces of stolen goods left there by the thieves, and the skeletons of several of their victims. Further remains were found buried under the cellar floor and in shallow graves about the garden. It seems that proof of the landlord's guilt was not finally established until 80 years after his death. Oddly, no-one remembers his name, and as far as we know his ghost has never been seen haunting the country roads.

HISTORICAL EMBROIDERIES AND LIGHTER TALES

The Devil of Bryn-y-wrach

Old Morgan was a colporteur, a bible hawker, who spent his days in the valleys of South Glamorgan. From Brynmenyn he would set off up the Ogmore Valley to Aberkenfig and follow the road north-east, passing through village after village until he reached Lewistown. There he would climb the winding path over Bryn-y-wrach to Llangeinor and wend his way down the Garw Valley back to his home in Brynmenyn. Whenever he was thirsty or weary he called at the taverns along the way for a mug of ale or a night's rest. And throughout the valleys he became a familiar sight, with his three-quarter coat, wide brimmed hat and satchel filled with black bound samples.

It was just at sunset one winter's day when he was climbing the slopes of Bryn-y-wrach. The sky was overcast and an icy wind swept down the mountain path. His legs grew weary and his satchel hung heavily on his shoulder. Then he saw the grey walls of Ael-y-bryn, a little hillside farm, and a thankful sigh escaped his lips.

'My old friend Elias John,' he muttered to himself, and he trudged on, anticipating a wholesome supper, a blazing log fire and a warm bed for the night.

At length he reached the farmhouse door and knocked upon it with his knobbly stick. It was the farmer's daughter Mair, a frosty uncharitable wench, who came to the doorway. She looked at the hawker coldly.

'Noswaith dda, fy ngeneth.' (Good evening, my young lady.) 'Tell your father that his old friend, Morgan, has called on his way to Llangeinor.'

'He's gone to the village and won't be back until long after nightfall,' Mair said sharply. Then the door was slammed in Morgan's face and he was left standing there, wearing a frown of indignation. With darkness fast falling and the wind biting through his shabby coat, the old hawker was too cold and weary to continue his journey over the mountain. So he decided to shelter in the barn and await the arrival of his old friend Elias John. He would never be so inhospitable.

For a time he shuffled about on the straw-strewn floor while the farmer's brown cow nuzzled around in the trough beside him. Presently he saw a bright glow when the lamps were lit in the farmhouse, and once he fancied he heard the sound of laughter coming from the kitchen. Curious, he crept over to the window and peered through the shutters. And there was the deceitful wench sitting at the table with Meredith, a field-hand whom, only last summer, Elias John had chased from the farm with a pitchfork for philandering with his daughter. He had dared him to set foot on his land again.

For a while they sat close together and then Mair brought a large pie from the oven and laid it before him. Next she brought two flagons of ale from the larder. Morgan licked his lips as the golden crust was broken. There was nothing he liked better than a freshly baked meat pie.

It was just then that the clip-clop of a horse's hoofs was heard on the cobble-stones. Mair was startled. She rushed about the kitchen wondering how to conceal the evidence of her young man's presence, for she well remembered her father's vow that if ever again Meredith was caught skulking around Bryn-y-wrach he would stake his carcass in the fields to scare away the crows.

It was hardly any time at all before Elias John's heavy footsteps crossed from the stable to the house. Mair rushed this way and that. The steaming pie was hidden beneath the pendulum in the grandfather clock; the flagons of ale were hurriedly concealed in the butter churn; and Meredith, with no time to escape, crouched out of sight inside a spacious boiler which stood in the corner.

Morgan called out in the dusky light. 'Elias John, my old friend. Sut ydych chi?' (How are you?)

They met at the doorway and the farmer recognised him at once.

'Morgan. Sut ydych chi? Come in, come in.'

He unlatched the door and led him into the kitchen.

'You must shelter here for the night. Warm yourself by the fire – this east wind cuts like a knife. Mair, a hot drink and a bite to eat for our guest.'

Morgan sat there with his feet in the hearth, watching the blazing logs flicker in the chimney. Mair scowled.

'There's only cheese and a piece of stale bread,' she said.

Together they sat in the lamplight, talking of old friends and happy times, and nibbling a little bread and cheese. All the while Mair's eyes darted to and from the boiler in the corner, but Meredith made no sound.

An hour passed. Elias John threw more logs on the fire while Morgan lit his pipe and talked on and on of Kitty Abergarw from Brynmenyn, of salmon fishing in the Ogmore, and of Mallt, the old hag who lived in her stone hut over the mountain. And when he told of how she, the 'Knowing One' had shown him the secret of her mysterious spells, Elias John's eyes lit up with enthusiasm. He drew his chair closer. 'Magic spells!' he whispered.

A mischievous smile wrinkled the corners of Morgan's mouth. 'You might wonder how she never starves, all alone there on the mountain.'

There was only the beat of the grandfather clock and the crackle of burning wood when Morgan raised his arms and, in solemn voice, recited Mallt's spell.

'Gwrando arnaf, o Yspryd y Mynydd,' (Hear me, Spirit of the Mountain,) he began with much volume. Then he took a handful of salt from the table and sprinkled it into the fire, gazing into the blue flames as he muttered the secret words.

At length the spell was cast. Morgan searched about the kitchen, first behind the little door of the grandfather clock and then inside the milk churn. Much to Mair's dismay and Elias John's astonishment, he returned to the table with two flagons of ale and a delicious meat pie.

They ate their supper with relish. Then, after exchanging a reminiscent tale or two, Morgan volunteered another demonstration of his strange powers. Old Mallt, he explained, had taught him a spell with which he could summon Satan himself.

'Arglwydd Mawr!' (Great God!), Elias John exclaimed, crossing himself, for he had no wish to encourage the Devil.

'He would never appear to good Christian folk,' Morgan assured him. 'But should he be seen on the slopes of Bryn-y-wrach, then you will know how to drive him off with the fear of God, and he will never darken your doorway again.'

So, with much trepidation, the farmer consented.

Once more Morgan raised his arms, and after calling 'Gwrando

arnaf, o Yspryd y Mynydd' many times, each with more volume than the last, he recited some sinister spell. This time he kindled the wood fire already laid beneath the boiler. The farmer's daughter stifled a cry and ran from the room.

'Take this stick,' said Morgan, 'and if Old Nick appears you must fill his black heart with terror, and banish him from this place!'

Minutes passed. The farmer watched anxiously as the flames licked around the bottom of the boiler. But Meredith still crouched silently inside.

'He knows he'll find no welcome here,' Elias John whispered.

Then, as the wood crackled and blue smoke curled toward the ceiling, a sound like the rumble of thunder was heard within the boiler. A moment later the lid flew off and, with a startled cry, the figure of Meredith sprang into view panting as though he had escaped the very fires of Hell. Through the smoke and the shadowy

46

light he rushed toward them. With an oath – and surprising alacrity for one his age – Elias John pursued him about the room, raining blows upon his head and shoulders with Morgan's knobbly stick. It was hardly any time at all before he had fled through the door and disappeared in the darkness.

'Arglwydd Mawr!' Elias John gasped when he had regained his composure. 'I would never have dreamt ... Arglwydd Mawr!' Then he gave a little chuckle. 'You know, Morgan, as he dashed past me in fright – and in the lamplight and all – he had the wicked look of that field-hand from over Bryn-y-wrach: the one I chased off last summer.'

That night Elias John slept with a clear conscience. Morgan curled up with a blanket on the chair by the fire. As for Mair, perhaps she cried herself to sleep.

The Victors' Chariot

Summer after summer the members of Ystalyfera's town band trudged homeward down the Cwmtwrch Valley, their heads hung low, their instruments tucked under their arms or slung over their shoulders. Each year it was the same old story: they returned from the eisteddfod at Cwmllynfell – disappointed. And with a wry smile their conductor, Morgan Rhys, would say, 'Na hitiwch, fechgyn. Gwell lwc tro nesa.' (Never mind, boys. Better luck next time.)

Their luck changed in the summer of 1850. On the day of the competition they made their way along the canal towpath to the Gurnos Basin.* There the path began its long slope up the valley. Beside them ran the black incline along which the trams ran from the colliery. Specks of coal dust glistened in the morning sun. It was a long climb and they tramped along in silence one behind the other. As usual Morgan Rhys led the way, his jacket over his arm, his tie all askew. Halfway up the valley they stopped for a rest, and as they sat beside the path Morgan rubbed his hands and said, 'Cofiwch fy ngheiriau, fechgyn. Y flwyddyn hon yr ydym yn mynd i ennill.' (Mark my words, boys. This year we're going to win.)

From villages all over the valley folk gathered at Cwmllynfell for the annual eisteddfod. All day long the sweet sound of music and song lingered on the hillsides.

There was an air of confidence about Morgan as he mounted the platform and stood before his band. They had selected an arrangement of the old Welsh hymn 'Bryn Calfaria'. The harmony of euphoniums and trombones, the clarion notes of the cornet and the resonant beat of the drum held the audience spellbound. On this special occasion the musicians of Ystalyfera played with rare inspiration and, as Morgan had predicted, late that afternoon the trophy was theirs.

As evening wore on there was much celebration. Time and again the silver cup was filled with mead, and ale flowed freely. A merrier band of performers had never been seen in Cwmllynfell. They went

* The Gurnos Basin was used to turn barges laden with coal on route from the colliery to the docks.

lurching down through the valley, their instruments slung about them, laughing together and singing snatches of old Welsh hymns. But the Cwmtwrch Valley stretched far before them. After a long day and an evening of revelry they soon grew weary.

Presently they came to the tram-way which sloped down to the Gurnos Basin. It was Morgan Rhys who noticed the empty tram standing at the top of the incline. He scrambled up the mound of slag which had been tipped beside the rails.

'Cerbyd i'r ennillwyr!' (A chariot for the victors!) he called, for he thought it would be quicker than walking down the rocky path, and far less exhausting. The others followed – all except one, for he could not manage the steep climb up the slag heap with his big base drum.

At leisurely pace the tram started to trundle along the track, filled to capacity with members of the band. They were all in high spirits, shouting and roaring with laughter, with the shrill notes of the cornet heralding their descent. Farther along the incline their 'chariot' gathered speed. Morgan pulled on the brake. A trail of sparks flew from the rails, but the tram careered on, gaining speed at an alarming rate. In a little while the end of the track was in sight. 'Arglwydd mawr!' (Great God!) they exclaimed.

Several jumped over the side, their fall cushioned by banks of coal dust. The rest of the band, with trombones, tubas and euphoniums were hurtled into the Gurnos Basin. No-one was seriously hurt, but for a long time the silver cup they won at Cwmllynfell lay buried under the murky water.

The Mark of Cain

The village of Herbrandston lies a few miles to the west of Milford Haven in the old county of Pembrokeshire. And there, peacefully situated beside the village green, stands the old Norman church of St Mary the Virgin.

It is well known throughout the county that everyone belonging to this little church is specially blessed, even though some of the congregation come from neighbouring parishes. Many believe that they have divine protection from violent death, for at the end of the First World War the 24 men who had served in the armed forces all returned safely. Among them was the local squire and the rector's two sons. This rare phenomenon was repeated in 1945 when the 43 men and women who answered the call to duty returned unscathed to the village of Herbrandston. Many of them had been in action in dangerous theatres of war, on land, sea and in the air.

It is said to be the only parish in the whole of the United Kingdom where no-one was killed in two World Wars. On Armistice Sunday the parishioners of Herbrandston remember the fallen from towns and villages throughout the county, and offer prayers of thanksgiving for the special blessing bestowed on members of St Mary the Virgin.

It is likely that this guardian angel has watched over the parish for centuries, for a tomb believed to be that of a crusader who escaped death in the Holy Wars lies in a niche in the church.

Stranger still is the story of the marble cross which marks a grave in the churchyard. In 1875, Phillip Carrol Walker, a young lieutenant in the Royal Artillery, was stationed in a fort nearby. One night after a battalion dinner there was much drinking and revelry. A bitter quarrel ensued between two fellow officers. Then, in a drunken rage, they fought, and the young lieutenant was stabbed.

The murder trial caused quite a sensation in the county, especially when the accused officer was acquitted. Local people considered the verdict outrageous. It gave rise to a saying which became popular throughout the county. Whenever someone was in desperate plight with no hope of survival folk said, 'Only a Pembrokeshire jury can save him now.'

51

The young officer was buried behind the church of St Mary the Virgin. Hidden beneath the ivy on his tombstone is the simple inscription: 'Phillip Carrol Walker, Lt., R.A. Died 28th May, 1875. Aged 26 years.'

Over the years many people have visited the churchyard at Herbrandston to witness an inexplicable manifestation. In the summer of 1875 there appeared on the marble headstone the clear outline of a hand holding a dagger. This remained indelible despite attempts to wash it away. Geologists tell of selective weathering in the metamorphic limestone which left a blemish of quaint shape. But the old folk of the village believe to this day that it is a divine mark of retribution.

There Was An Old Woman

One day, many years ago, a gentleman from England came to visit a mining village set among the hills of the Afan Valley. In those days the village was seldom honoured with visitors of high station. No-one remembers the nature of his business there, nor why he had chosen to travel on the Great Western Railway, since most gentlemen of position had chauffeur-driven motor cars. Because it was a winter night, perhaps the mountain roads were coated with frost and snow drifts. But there he was, in fine tailored clothes, sitting in the waiting room of a small railway station, with half an hour to spare until the arrival of the evening train which would take him back to his metropolis in the east. Beside him sat a pinched-faced servant who had accompanied him on the journey.

They were listening to the wind howling in the chimney when the door opened and a chill draught blew into the room. A strange looking man – a familiar character among the village folk – came in and hastily closed the door behind him. He shuffled around the room, first this way, then that, and finally stood at the window where he could peep up and down the platform. Then he went over to the fireplace and looked solemnly at the gentleman and his companion.

'Where is she? Which way did she go?' he whispered.

The gentleman frowned and his servant fidgeted uneasily in his seat. Furtively the stranger's eyes darted about the room. He was a little, gaunt figure wrapped in shabby clothes; a shapeless hat, a muffler knotted around his neck, a drab raincoat. His voice had a melodious lilt.

'She's hiding somewhere, waiting for me in a dark corner!'

He turned the gas light low and listened for a while. Then he sat between the two visitors, looking from one to the other as he told them his tale of an old woman who pursued him through the darkness. His captive audience watched the flames flicker in the fire.

'A cunning old witch! Steals behind me in the moonlight wherever I go. A horrid grey face with burning eyes, following me over the mountain-side and through the valley ...'

He paused for a moment to glance over his shoulder toward the

53

door. The visitors' eyes turned in the same direction, as though the door had opened and an old woman was standing there in the moonlight.

'She haunts me every hour of the darkness; knocks at my door, throws open my window and calls my name ...'

They sat there until the fire had burned low and the room became cold. And all the while the strange little man cursed the mysterious witch who haunted him relentlessly. So fearful was his voice and expression that once the servant fancied that there was a tapping on the window and that he heard the wind whispering words in the chimney.

The end of the story was breathed in a whisper.

'It's the train that frightens her away; that's why I hide here in the evenings. When the train comes thundering through the tunnel you'll hear her scream, just as she did one night long ago when she fell in its path!'

The train was late, and as the minutes passed by the gentleman tired of the senseless tale. Impatiently he stood up, looked at his pocket watch and studied the little man with some disdain.

At that moment a signal bell rang and a shrill whistle came from the tunnel. The fugitive trembled with fright and clutched at the gentleman's coat. As the train was heard approaching the station he clung to the gentleman desperately, flinging his arms about him and crying out in fear.

With the aid of his servant the gentleman managed to break free of the stranger's grasp. Then the three of them left the waiting room and went their separate ways. The visitors boarded their train while the fugitive ran off along the platform and disappeared in a cloud of steam released from the engine.

From the window of his 1st-class compartment this certain visitor of high station watched the Welsh hills pass by as the train passed through the Afan Valley. He amused himself with visions of a gaunt little man fleeing in terror along the mountain paths, with the ghost of an old woman at his heels.

It was when the ticket collector was looking at him over the rim of his spectacles that the smile vanished from his face. He was searching through his pockets for the ticket that was requested. With bitter regret he realised why a wily rustic had sought refuge in a dimly-lit waiting room; why he had clung to him in fear. Somewhere among the hills was a gaunt, little man with a stolen wallet and a gold watch hidden in the pocket of a shabby raincoat.

To this day many old folk of the village remember an artful character of years gone by. The railway station is no longer there, yet some say that if you listen carefully on a quiet night, a train can be heard whistling in the old tunnel. But no-one remembers an old woman with a grey face and burning eyes who haunts the mountain paths.

The Legend of Tresilian Cave

The ancient castle of St Donat's stands on the most southerly coast of Wales overlooking the Bristol Channel and the northern hills of Devon. In years gone by it was inhabited by the Stradling family, and today the body of Sir Henry Stradling lies buried there in a crypt under the chapel.

Sir Henry was reputed to be a smuggler and was known to indulge in a little piracy. He made many voyages to France where he picked up most of his contraband. It is said that one day while he was on such a voyage his ship was attacked by a Breton pirate. The ship was scuttled and left to sink with its cargo and crew aboard. Sir Henry was seized and held to ransom. A bitter and resentful captive, he remained in the hands of the pirates until the Stradling family paid a large sum of money for his release.

He never forgot the indignities he suffered during his captivity. For a long time he was vengeful, and from a high tower he had built in his castle he kept a constant watch along the shore from St Athan to St Bride's.

His vigil was finally rewarded when, one evening, his retainers noticed a strange ship moored in the bay and a solitary raider

standing on the shore. It was thought that either by design or misfortune he had been left behind, for when he was seized by Sir Henry's retainers the ship was seen sailing away.

It might have been a twist of fate that marooned him there, because when he was bound and brought to the castle Sir Henry's eyes glittered with hate. Standing there before him was the Breton pirate who had captured him on the high sea and murdered his crew.

Sir Henry's vengence was fearful. The pirate was taken to the mouth of Tresilian Cave beneath the castle walls. There he was buried in the sand until only his head and shoulders were uncovered. No-one knows the terror that possessed him as he listened to the waves crash upon the beach and watched the relentless tide sweep toward the cave.

How many thousand tides have come and gone since that time! But to this day whenever a winter wind blows in from the sea shrill cries of fright and despair are heard echoing through Tresilian Cave.

The Stradling family came to an abrupt end in 1738. It is said that one of the family was murdered within the castle and that the figure of a stately old lady dressed in the clothes of long ago appeared there from time to time, and ghostly wails came from behind the castle walls.

Nowadays the castle houses an Outward Bound college for international students and is hardly a likely setting for a haunting. Yet even today when the castle stands black against the night sky and the wind moans through Tresilian Cave, many old folk will not pass by.

True Love

Our love story ended at a graveside in the churchyard at Llanguicke, a little church which stands among the hills of Pontardawe. It began 16 years earlier in a farmhouse nearby, for it was there that a baby girl was born to the shepherd and his wife. Sadly, her mother died while she was still a child, so the shepherd was left alone to tend the sheep and care for his treasured daughter. Her name was Rosamund, and he loved her above all else in the world.

Time passed, and Rosamund became a beautiful girl with soft, golden hair and eyes as blue as the sky. Her happy smile was like a ray of sunshine and won the heart of many a young man in the village. But no-one admired her more than David, a young shepherd boy. From the first day he came to work at her father's farm, he roamed the hills with his shepherd's crook, dreaming only of her. Each day, just at noon, she met him in a craggy dell with food she had prepared for his meal. It was there that they fell in love.

One night when the moon shone on the hillside, they lay in a bed of soft heather and swore to be true, one to the other.

'Until the day I die,' said Rosamund, looking up at the stars.

'For always and always, until the end of time,' David vowed.

But, as often happens, the path of true love has many a cruel twist. Rosamund's father had long since dreamed of the time when his daughter would marry a man of wealth and position, for there was no-one fairer than she in all the Swansea Valley. Her love for a humble shepherd boy filled his heart with bitterness. Once he decided to send him away, but he feared that then he would lose Rosamund, too, and that was more than he could bear. So day by day, and through sleepless nights, a wicked plot crept into his thoughts.

Cunningly, he bided his time. Then, one evening, he stole down to the river, where some travelling tinkers were sitting around a camp fire. He sat among them until the fire burned low. No-one heard the whispers nor the swelling of angry voices that went on there. But, at length, silver coins were greedily accepted and the tinkers were well content.

The next day David did not come to the dell where he and

Rosamund usually met. She roamed the hills, but there was no sign
of him. He had disappeared. It was a mystery no-one could explain.
Nowadays the story is told of a shepherd boy who was abducted by
tinkers, and hidden in a caravan travelling along the coast road.
There, it is said, they came upon a band of pirates who had come
ashore to steal and plunder and had taken him away across the sea.

As the months drew by, Rosamund's heart was breaking. There
was no longer a smile on her lips and the sparkle had gone from her
eyes. Through the bitter winds of winter she wandered alone over
the hills. Her tears were now all shed, and a lingering sadness came
upon her. Before the heather bloomed the next summer she fell ill

with a fever and died, for she had no-one to live for.

The summer passed and winter came. It was never known how it came about, but one day David returned to his native village. He was seen in the churchyard where Rosamund lay, his face drawn and pale with grief. He knelt beside her grave, and there he whispered again the vow he had made on the hillside.

Over the years, he came many times to the churchyard at Llanguicke. Always he knelt silently at the graveside. Then, late one summer evening, the rector saw a figure standing there. He thought it strange that the light of the moon shone right through it. When he looked again, the figure had vanished. One moment it was there, the next it had gone.

Nowadays, folk say that if you walk through the moonlit churchyard you may see the ghost of a young shepherd who haunts the grave of his true love. And if he keeps the vow he made in a craggy dell, he will appear there for always and always, until the end of time.

A different version of this tale has a more dramatic ending:

One day, after many months of voyaging along the southern coast, a shepherd boy, dressed in the clothes of a seafaring man, returned to his true love. When he learned of her death he was beside himself with grief. And in the churchyard at Llanguicke he hanged himself from the branch of a yew tree. He was buried somewhere in the hills, but time and again his ghost appeared there above the gravestones.

In an attempt to rid his church of this gruesome spectre, the rector ordered that the tree be chopped down. For a long time afterwards the ghost was never seen. Then, one night when the churchyard was lit with moonlight, an old man of the village was passing by. He tells of the ghost of a young man which appeared, swaying from side to side above the ground, just at the place where the tree ónce stood.

But it was a cold, winter night and he had taken a drink or two to protect himself from the chill of the frosty air.

Devil in the Treetop

One autumn morning, long before sunrise, a nobleman from the south coast of Glamorgan was wending his way home after a merry evening at Cardiff Castle where each year a grand costume ball was held to celebrate the eve of All Saints Day. There had been much jollity and the wine and mead had flowed freely.

He dozed in the saddle as his horse trotted along the moonlit way, with no sound to be heard other than the occasional cry of the screech-owl and the rhythmic tread of the horse's hoofs.

An awesome sight he would have appeared to anyone passing by, for he was wearing a costume in the likeness of the devil himself, with a fearful mask to hide his face, a black, scaled skin clinging to his body and a curled tail behind.

The gentle rocking motion of his journey and the effect of drink lulled the rider into a fitful sleep. His head fell on to his chest, and as his steed rounded a bend he fell headlong from the saddle and rolled into the heather at the roadside. He awoke with an oath only to see his mount canter off into the woodland.

The nobleman, in his satanic disguise, hurried in pursuit, but already the sound of the animal's hoofs had faded in the distance. It was then that he saw several figures emerge from a shadowy grove into the moonlight.

In those days villagers on the south coast were often terrorised by raiding pirates who came to poach and pillage. Cattle were slaughtered and carried off, dwellings burned, and inhabitants murdered or captured and taken into slavery. The nobleman knew that he could expect no mercy and that he was in great peril.

Fearing that the raiders would discover him, he hid in the branches of a tree. There he watched as they came nearer and listened to their cruel laughter. A brace of deer was trussed to a bough and carried on their shoulders.

By some strange chance they rested under the very tree in which he was hiding. There they gathered wood and built a fire and roasted fowl on a crude spit, counting their loot as the wood crackled.

In the branches above them not a leaf stirred. The fugitive saw the

flames glow and the smoke curl upward into the darkness. It burned his eyes and filled his lungs and made his head reel. Then, with a startled cry, he fell from the branches on to the fire below.

There he danced like the devil ascending from hell, his clothes afire, his arms raised in alarm, trampling amid the sparks and blue clouds of smoke with cloven hoofs. As he rushed furiously among a tangle of flaming boughs, the hideous face and horns of Lucifer shone in the firelight.

Before sunrise on that autumn morning, shrill cries of terror were heard as a band of brigands fled through the woods and bracken. And it is said that they never once looked back until, breathless with fright and exhaustion, they reached the chill waters of the Bristol Channel.

Mansell's Ghost

Rhosili Bay on the western end of the Gower Peninsula has always been a dangerous place for seafarers. In rough weather the prevailing winds sweep across the Bristol Channel, carrying fierce waves toward the shore. There are, too, the craggy rocks of Worms Head* lying to the south of the bay and the treacherous Burry Holms to the north.

On stormy nights during the 17th century two treasure ships – one Spanish, one Portuguese – sank off the shores of Rhosili. Moidores, doubloons and Peruvian dollars were found on the beach between 1770 and 1840 when the sands had receded. One wreck was looted by the local people who carried its treasure off to their cottage homes.

At that time there lived in the village of Rhosili a Squire Mansell, a member of a prominent local family, and well remembered as a tyrant. When news of the wreck's precious cargo reached the Squire, immediately his interest was aroused. He charged across the beach with his coach and horses and drove away the peasants, seizing for himself the lion's share of the treasure trove. Then he pursued them to their homes and confiscated the gold and silver coins they had hidden there.

* Worms Head, the majestic rock formation that marks the western tip of Gower, resembles a huge sea serpent. The name is derived from the Old English 'wurm' meaning dragon.

In the years that followed, nothing further was heard of him. Folk say that he went across the sea to Ireland where he squandered his fortune on drink and immoral living. Then, so the story goes, when all his money was spent he returned to his family in Gower. Many a time he was seen at ebb tide galloping across Rhosili Bay in a coach drawn by four black horses. But the shifting sands had long since smothered the wreck, and whatever treasure remained was buried forever.

Nowadays the two-mile stretch of beach from Worms Head to Burry Holms is little changed. On a summer day hang-gliders join the seagulls as they drift from the heights of Rhosili Down toward the holiday makers below.

Sometimes, when the tide is at its farthest ebb and the moon is bright, the ghost of Squire Mansell* goes thundering over the beach in a coach drawn by four black chargers. From north to south and south to north he goes, in a futile search for a treasure which lies buried in the sand.

* Many campers at the caravan site below the northern slopes of Rhosili Down have seen and heard the ghostly coach and horses galloping over the moonlit sands. The old folk of the village remember the popular game 'Mansell's Ghost' which they played as children. They raced down the hillside through the ferns, four charging steeds at the head, with a coach and driver trailing behind.

The Black Legion

To the west of Fishguard Bay along the north coast of Dyfed stands Carregwasted Point, midway between Strumble Head and Goodwick. There, in that rocky cove, you will find an inscription written in English and Welsh on an upright stone: 'Memorial of the Landing of the French, February 22, 1797.' The story of this 'invasion' is well known among the folk of Pembrokeshire – that little England beyond Wales.

Near the end of the 18th century the French Republic was confident that the combined strength of the Spanish and French fleets would overwhelm the British warships and pave the way for the conquest of the British Isles. With King George's front-line defences crippled in the English Channel, he would be powerless to withstand an invasion. So the French planned to terrorise the enemy with a brutal raid on the west coast. This marauding force, comprising mainly of several hundred convicts and galley slaves,* wore dark-coloured uniforms and called themselves the Black Legion.

On February 17, 1797 they set sail from Brest in four vessels under the command of an American Colonel, renowned as an adventurer. His orders were to pillage and burn selected cities on the western coast, spreading terror among the peasant folk.

In the Bristol Channel the raiders came upon a British warship† and instantly abandoned their plan to attack the city of Bristol. They made all speed westward into St George's Channel. Here they sailed north, rounded Strumble Head off the tip of Pembrokeshire, and finally anchored off Carregwasted Point. The 'fearless' Black Legion pulled ashore to prepare for their mission of plunder and murder.

Their vessels had been seen by the villagers of Llanwnda who raised the alarm. Lord Cawdor, an aristocrat of the area, mustered

---

* Although convicts and galley slaves seem unlikely conscripts for such a venture, it is recorded that they were promised freedom and reward on successful completion of their mission.

† Historians claim that the ship sighted by the raiders was more than likely an unarmed packet-boat bound for Dublin.

the local volunteers who advanced to meet the raiders. The women of the village, anxious to see the outcome of the encounter, followed their menfolk toward the shore. Their red flannel shawls were wrapped about them for the wind was cold.

The volunteers were heavily outnumbered, but they moved forward resolutely. At the crest of Carregwasted Point the raiders' commander hesitated. He was not deterred by the gallant band of volunteers, but beyond them, some distance to their rear, he saw what he thought to be the red coats of the regular infantry. Trapped between the sea and what he imagined to be a company of redcoats, the Colonel's Black Legion laid down their arms and surrendered unconditionally to Lord Cawdor.

The mystery of the French surrender at Carregwasted Point has never been solved. Historians cannot accept the legend of the women wrapped in their red shawls, but it is no more incredible than the adventures of the Black Legion.

The Lady

In years gone by Candleston Castle stood in splendour among the Merthyr Mawr warren of sand dunes. To the north were the hills and the vales where the rivers Llwynfi, Garw and Ogmore met and flowed past the castle to the limestone cliffs and the sea beyond.

The legend of The Lady goes back to one spring morning many hundreds of years ago. In the courtyard of the castle, the domain of the Norman Baron De Londres, knights and gentry with their attendant servants gathered for a morning hunt. Among them was Hawies, a beautiful young lady of humble birth.

In a corner of the courtyard she came upon a peasant who was chained to the wall and gazed up at the high wisps of cloud. Hawies spoke to him with compassion. When asked why he looked up at the sky, he replied, 'I want to remember the golden sun and the blue of the heavens.' At the end of the day he was to suffer the cruel punishment of the Baron De Londres. For the last time he would watch the sun fall behind the hills, for at sundown his eyes would be burned and he would be plunged forever into a world of darkness.

As she stood beside the prisoner, the Baron appeared on his black stallion.

'My lord,' she called as he passed by. 'Have mercy on a poor peasant. The deer he stole was food for his children.'

The Baron paused. His eyes were cold, unyielding.

Hawies pleaded. 'My lord, they have nowhere to find meat for their families. Give them land where they may freely hunt for themselves.'

'Then you shall be their champion,' the Baron mocked. 'As far as you walk barefoot from sunrise to sunset, that land shall be theirs.'

He laughed and dug his heels in the horse's flanks.

The next morning at first light Hawies set off on her journey. She travelled over a stretch of downs and woodland to the south-east.

The castle walls were far behind her when she forded the chill water of the Ogmore river and climbed the hills which rose 300 feet above the river bank. Breathless, she struggled on through wood and glade, over grassy hill and sandy mound. She stumbled over sharp rocks and fell to her knees. Her feet were burned and blistered, but

her blood-stained footfalls went on and on, measuring mile after weary mile.

When the sun sank over the sea, Hawies lay exhausted in a bed of heather.

From that day, and for many a year, the beautiful stretch of land from Candleston Castle to the village of Southerndown became common ground, where peasants could wander and hunt freely.

Even today local folk refer to that area on the south coast of Wales as The Lady, and if ever you chance to roam in the footsteps of Hawies look carefully for the bare patches of ground, for there, it is said, the limestone rock is tainted red where once the bloody feet of a lady trod.

A few stones of Candleston Castle still remain. No-one knows the fate of the cruel Baron De Londres. But if you journey a little farther to the north to the village of Ewenny, you will come upon a quaint priory which the Baron built there for the sake of his soul in the hereafter.

SUPERNATURAL TALES

FAIRIES AND WITCHES

The Legend of Llyn Barfog*

Barfog Lake is cradled in rocky hills which lie to the west of the main coastal highway near the northern border of Dyfed. And there, long years ago, lived a farmer who tilled the soil and led his cattle to pasture in the lowland of Cwm Dyffryn Gwyn. It is said that there was no shrewder judge of livestock from the Cambrian Mountains to the Brecon Beacons.

Throughout the valley, tales were told of the Gwragedd Annwn, the noble dames of Fairyland, who sometimes appeared on the banks of Llyn Barfog in the first rays of sunlight. They walked beside the water-lilies, while grazing nearby were a few handsome fairy cows which accompanied them.

Early one summer morning, when the farmer was in the hills, he saw for himself the Gwragedd Annwn strolling at the water's edge. Their cattle wandered to the rich grass on the hillside. From his hiding place among the heather he watched the fairy folk pass by and looked with admiration at their fine animals, all chocolate and white, with sturdy limbs and sad eyes. He rose from the heather and crept toward them. But the moment the grass stirred at his feet the Gwragedd Annwn glided into the lake and vanished beneath the surface. The cows raised their heads and first one and then another disappeared into the water. But the third cow had strayed farther away and did not hear his approach. The farmer chased the frightened beast down into the valley, and before the morning was over it was tethered in his byre.

From that day onward the farmer's fortunes changed. His fairy cow gave milk so rich in quality that his dairy produce was the

* It is thought that Llyn Barfog (the Bearded Lake) derives its name from the water-lilies which cover the surface of the water. Some say that it commemorates a noble deed performed in the area by one of King Arthur's knights who was known as 'the bearded one'.

wonder of the county. From the far-south of Cardigan, from Merioneth and Montgomery folk came to buy their cheese and butter.

Many summers passed, and each year the cow's progeny multiplied, until the farmer at Cwm Dyffryn Gwyn had the finest herd of cattle in all the valleys of Wales. Unlike mortal beasts, it seemed that their function as milch-kine and calf bearers would go on forever. 'It's the beast of the Gwragedd Annwn!' his neighbours would say ruefully.

And so their jealousy and bitterness grew.

Late one night, when the farmer was asleep, stealthy footfalls approached the byre across the cobbled yard. No-one heard the large iron key turn in the door nor the chain jingle as the farmer's precious cow was untethered and taken from its stall. The animal was led out into the moonlight and along the hillside path toward Llyn Barfog. And there it disappeared beneath the water-lilies from where it had emerged many summers ago.

Throughout that night the cattle were restive. In the byre young bulls bellowed and tore the earth with their stamping hoofs. When dawn came the farmer was distressed to discover the empty stall. The herd was put out to pasture while he set off in search of the missing cow. But they turned from the meadow and wound their way up the craggy hillside. Along the path they went, one behind the other, all the progeny of Y Fuwch Gyfeiliorn (the Stray Cow), lowing and snorting and quickening their stride as though some magic spell was beckoning them. From the hill-top the farmer saw them approach Llyn Barfog. In a little while they were gone forever.

For the rest of his days the old farmer rose at first light. Although he kept close watch on the banks of the lake there was never a sign of the Gwragedd Annwn nor their fairy beasts. But there are folk thereabouts who believe that one of the cow's descendants did not return to Llyn Barfog, for today the farms around Cwm Dyffryn Gwyn still produce the finest milk and butter in West Wales.

The Old Hag of the Mountains

Long ago there was an old woman who wandered from place to place around the Vale of Ewyas and the villages beneath the Black Mountains. No-one knew her name or where she came from, so she was known as the Old Hag of the Mountains, for it was believed that when she was weary she laid her head to rest in a cave among the mountains.

She lived mainly on potatoes and turnips which she stole from the fields. Occasionally the fleece and bones of sheep she had slaughtered and the ashes of a log fire were found in the caves. Come summer or winter she always looked the same, with long, dark clothes and a black shawl over her shoulders. And through the woods and meadows she roamed, calling at farmhouses and cottages, peddling charms and garlands of wild flowers, and telling the fortunes of those who would spare her a penny.

Many a strange tale is told of the Old Hag of the Mountains. The

following accounts of her witchcraft were gathered by children from that quiet county of Brecknock (now Powys).

One evening, late on in the summer, two farm workers near the village of Pandy were leaving the fields after their day's work when they saw the figure of a woman dressed in black standing all alone on the heath. Her shoulders were bent and her head was turned to one side looking up at the clouds. They heard her croaky voice reciting a spell, and when she raised her arms the sky went dark and the corn field tossed and swayed in a sudden wind. Then a fierce storm came over the Black Mountains.

All through that night lightning lit up the valley and thundery rain swelled the streams. Before morning the heath and farm lands south of Wiral Woods lay under flood. The farmer was distressed to see his crops ruined. But the old hag chuckled to herself, for she well remembered how all summer long he had set his dogs on her whenever she was found trespassing in his fields.

It was late in the afternoon and dusk had fallen when the rector came upon the Old Hag of the Mountains just beyond Llanthony church.* She was standing alone outside the churchyard.

In a little while he was astonished to see misty shapes emerge from the shadows among the graves. The ghostly coven formed a circle with the old hag at its centre. There was a muttering of voices as they gathered together, and all the while the pale light of the moon shone right through them.

The rector crossed himself and hurried from the churchyard. When he arrived home he burned a candle in the window and tied a piece of red ribbon to his daughter's crib to protect the child from evil spirits.

One day some children from the village of Llanthony were playing together in Wiral Woods which lies at the foot of the Black Mountains. Shafts of sunlight came slanting down through the foliage. They hadn't noticed how quiet the woods had become for a

* Llanthony Church takes its name from the Welsh Llanddewi Nant Honddu – 'St David's church by the Honddu stream'. St David, patron saint of Wales, is thought to have spent part of his life there in the 6th century. The church, which dates from the 12th century, may occupy the site of his monastic cell. The church was so aligned that the altar faced directly toward the rising sun on March 1, St David's Day. During the Middle Ages the building served as a hospital for the priory and the surrounding district. Today it is the parish church and services are held there every Sunday.

summer's day – there were no birds singing; no woodpeckers tap-tapping in the boughs.

Presently an old woman came along the woodland path. She walked with a stoop, and a black shawl was draped over her shoulders. 'It's the Old Woman of the Mountains,' a girl whispered. 'Hag!' shouted one of the boys. 'Old Witch!' called another.

The old woman peered into the trees. Her face was withered. Her eyes burned. The children continued to taunt her from their hiding place, but when she shuffled closer they ran off, out of the shadow of the woods and across the meadow toward Landor's House.*

At length the children entered the copse where the ruins stood, and the old woman was nowhere in sight. Nothing but a crow was seen, flying low over the meadow behind them. Presently it perched on a wall of the ruined house. Its sharp eyes and hooked beak and angry squawk reminded them so of the old woman that they ran off again in fright.

Through wood and meadow they fled, with the crow swooping and soaring about them, until they came in sight of the priory walls. There the bird gave up its pursuit and circled overhead for a while. The next moment it was gone.

Beneath the remaining arches of the priory they stood, breathless and afraid. As they looked back toward the copse they saw that the crow had gone from the sky, and the figure of an old woman with a black shawl wrapped about her was moving away across the meadow in the direction of the Black Mountains.†

Sometimes in winter when snowdrifts lay on the hills a shepherd led his sheep to pasture in the Vale of Ewyas. One day a withered old woman crossed his path. His collie snapped at her heels and, with an oath, the shepherd sent her on her way, for he well remembered how sheep had strayed from the flock or disappeared from the fold, never to be seen again. The old woman stared long and hard at the shepherd as he plodded on down into the valley.

From that day on, whenever he descended the mountain path on his way to pasture, his sheep were tormented by a large crow which

---

* These ruins, hidden in a copse, are the remains of a house built by Walter Savage Landor, a writer who was a contemporary of Shelley, Byron and Wordsworth.

† It has always been believed that witches and evil spirits are loath to enter holy places and that they haven't the power to follow a person any farther than the middle of the next running stream.

screamed and squawked among the flock, sending them scurrying this way and that. The shepherd would wave his crook and call and whistle while his collie rushed around them in confusion. This wild chase would continue down the mountain side and across the meadow until the sheep had scampered over a stream to the north of Wiral Woods. There the crow would fly away to the west and disappear among the trees.

The Ox of Eynonsford Farm

The village of Reynoldston lies below the southern slopes of Cefn Bryn, the range of hills which form the backbone of the Gower Peninsula, running west from Three Cliffs Bay toward the Whitford Sands. Near the village police station you will find a path leading south in the direction of Penrice Woods. If you follow this path for a quarter of a mile you will come upon a solitary farmhouse, now much modernised to serve the needs of the 20th century but bearing the name it was given more than 200 years ago.

Eynonsford Farm was originally a long-house* with rough stone walls and a thatched roof. The present inhabitants, an old lady and her widowed daughter, and many old folk of the village, recall a tale which was told them by their forbears.

One summer's night long ago the farmer who lived there was awakened by the sound of strange music coming from the cattle stalls which were attached to the end of his kitchen. It was a haunting tune, unlike any he had heard before. Stealthily he made his way through the passageway which divided the dwelling rooms and the animal stalls. And there, in the glow of lantern light, he was astonished to see a host of Verry Volk† (Fairy Folk) dancing on the back of his favourite ox. A host of others, all in scarlet gowns, piped and reeled around the pebbled floor.

The merrymaking went on for a long time. At length the music stopped and the farmer watched, dismayed, as his ox was fed a mixture of rare herbs and fell dead before his eyes. The Verry Volk swarmed over the beast's body and stripped the hide from its back. Then they cut its flesh into 1,000 pieces and laid the bones on the

---

* The long-house, typical of farm buildings of the 16th-18th century, occupied both the family and its cattle. The dwelling area (pen uchaf) comprised two living rooms on the ground floor and two bedrooms above. The other part of the building was the cow-house and stable (pen isaf). A common entrance doorway led into a passage (y pen-llawr) serving both man and beast and wide enough to admit long-horned cattle. The floors of y pen-llawr and pen uchaf were paved with local stone slabs, while the floors of the pen isaf were part earth and part pitched with river pebbles. Above the pen isaf was a loft for hay, and nearby stood the peat-house. Furnishing was sparse and simple and the windows were unglazed. An old long-house from the county of Powys is preserved at the Welsh Folk Museum at St Fagans, Cardiff.

† The people of Gower refer to fairies as the 'Verry Volk'.

byre floor. Although he was much distressed, the farmer dare not interfere for he was afraid to offend the Verry Volk whose vengeance was always swift and terrible.

Beside a fairy knoll on the heath nearby they built a fire and roasted the meat over the flames. There their feasting and dancing continued well into the night, with the sounds of laughter and soft music.

When their merrymaking was over the Verry Volk returned to the byre and busily set about their task of reassembling the ox's bones. Piece by piece the beast took shape and in a little while its skeleton stood among them. Next they began to replace the hide, draping it like a shroud over the animal's frame.

It was just then that voices were raised in anger and the little folk searched around the byre floor for a bone which was missing from the ox's foreleg. They scurried this way and that, but although they searched high and low it was nowhere to be found.

Before the first light of dawn showed above Cefn Bryn, the Verry Volk had gone and had left the byre in darkness. At length the farmer ventured into the stall. He re-lit the lantern and there in the corner, its head bent over the feeding trough, stood his favourite ox. The beast turned to look at the farmer with its sad, brown eyes. A stalk of hay hung from its muzzle, and the beast looked as well and contented as ever.

Many a time the farmer told of the strange happenings that night at Eynonsford Farm. But there was no-one who would believe him. 'It was all a dream,' folk would say. But everyone thought it odd that from that day until the day it died the old ox was lame in the foreleg and always walked with a limp.

Old Hannah

One summer evening a farmer and his young daughter were travelling home from the fair at Haverfordwest. The cart trundled along toward the sunset, its wheels rattling on the bumpy road. Lying there with her head resting on a bundle of hay, the girl closed her eyes. After a while she fell asleep.

They were approaching Walton West when an old woman appeared at the roadside. Her hair was scraggy grey and her shoulders were hunched under a long, black shawl. The horse shied as she stepped in its path and the farmer pulled on the reins.

'Can you give a tired old woman a ride home?' she croaked.

The farmer nodded. Then the old woman lifted her skirts and hauled herself on to the back of the cart, where she sat down beside the young girl.

They jogged along for another mile or more before the girl opened her eyes and saw her sitting there. She watched the old woman wringing her gnarled hands and listened to the strange words she muttered to herself. The old woman's eyes were small and bright.

'Hannah, the witch!' the girl whispered, sitting up with a start, for tales of Hannah were well known around Walton West.

'Don't be afraid,' the old woman said. 'Hannah would never harm an innocent child.'

81

'Do you cast magic spells?' the girl asked. There was a spark of interest in her eyes.

Hannah chuckled.

Just then they came upon three teams harrowing in a field.

'Could you stop those teams with a magic spell?' the girl asked mischievously.

Old Hannah whispered a spell, and in a moment the horses of the first team reared in the shafts as though a wall of flame had flared up before them. The second team also shied suddenly, and the farm boy who was holding the reins fled, stumbling over the furrows. But the third team went harrowing along, unaffected by Hannah's spell.

The girl watched expectantly. Hannah peered over the side of the cart and then she said, 'My spell could never stop the third team, for the driver has a piece of mountain ash fast to his whip.'

The girl's father flicked the horse's flank, and the cart went rattling on toward Walton West.

The Vengeance of the Verry Volk

For more than 500 years the castle at Pennard has lain smothered in sand and overlooking Three Cliffs Bay and the valley of Parkmill. Today only the twin towers, the single arched gateway and part of the northern wall can be seen standing on a rubble bank. Its southern curtain wall has fallen. The communal hall, store rooms and private retiring room, typical of the Norman period, lie buried in the sand. And nearby are the scanty remains of what is said to be the former parish church. Archaeologists describe how fierce dust storms of the 13th century engulfed the castle. But the old folk of the village have a different story to tell.

One summer evening in the days of long ago the lord of Pennard Castle was celebrating his forthcoming marriage. There was a great feast and much revelry. Festivities were at their height when a look-out from the tower reported strange lights he had seen near the castle wall.

Under the cover of darkness the lord and his retainers crept from the castle to investigate this strange happening. In a tree-clad dell a ring of torches flickered and the sound of haunting music came to them, for there in the hollow the Verry Volk were dancing. Suspecting that they were enemies, the lord and his men charged among them in drunken rage, with angry oaths and swords flashing.

Sadly, many of the Verry Volk were crushed beneath their trampling feet. The rest fled in terror to a fairy knoll, leaving behind their proud queen who stood defiantly before the lord.

'Cowardly mortal!' she exclaimed. 'You have wantonly attacked our innocent pastime, and for this you shall suffer our vengeance. Before the sun falls once more over the bay, your castle and township will be destroyed.'

Then there appeared in the torch-light glow a bent and toothless hag whose shoulders rocked with laughter.

At noon the following day clouds rolled in from the north-west, plunging the land into darkness. A fierce wind stirred the sea and threw clouds of sand into the air. For hours the storm raged, until at length the township and the castle lay buried in drifts of sand and the folk were smothered in a dusty tomb.

Today local people tell of the Gwrach y Rhibyn* who haunts the remains of Pennard Castle. Usually it takes the form of an old hag who screeches and wails about the crumbling walls on the eve of a death in the village or the onset of a westerly gale.

Nowadays the ruins of the castle and parish church are surrounded by a golf links. The story of the haunting banshee is well known among members.

Late one afternoon, not very long ago, weird cries were heard coming from behind the castle walls, and what appeared to be a sword glinted in the sunlight.

But on this occasion it was not the presence of a wizened hag. A golf fanatic, alone on a practice round, pulled a drive off the 6th tee and his ball lay among the castle ruins. Wails of anguish drifted over the sand dunes as he hacked away among the rubble. Since that time he has been known affectionately as Peter Gwrach y Rhibyn.

* A spirit who portends death and destruction.

The Witch's Curse

Old Trickitt lived a long time ago in a stone house beneath the windswept crests of the Brecon Beacons.* Folk say he was a hard man with little charity in his heart, although he would brave a winter blizzard to rescue his sheep from snow drifts on the craggy hills.

One evening a gipsy woman came to his door peddling charm stones she had gathered from the slopes of Pen y Fan and had washed in a mountain stream. Beside her stood a little boy, pale and scrawny and dressed in rags.

She took a few stones from her apron pocket and offered them to the shepherd.

'They will bring you fair weather and good fortune,' she said, and her dark eyes twinkled.

Old Trickitt clutched the scruff of his growling collie and sent her on her way with harsh words.

'Then just a crust of bread for the little one,' she begged as he strode after her.

---

* The Brecon Beacons take their name from their use as sites for signal fires in days gone by.

He set his dog free and watched the child cry with fright while the woman kicked at its bared teeth. Then as they backed away through the rustic gate the gipsy looked long and hard at old Trickitt, and her eyes burned with hate.

Far off in a cave among the Beacons, while her boy lay curled asleep by a fire, the gipsy woman began a devilish recipe for an image of the cruel shepherd.

Her witch-doll had for its skin the burned body of a rat and for its hands and feet the limbs of a toad. For its body rare herbs were plucked from the mountain-side then left to smoulder on a special flat stone. For the doll's bones she chipped white quartz from a high cliff and gathered weeds from a neglected garden for sinews and muscles. Then, finally, salt water worms, pine gum and the heart of a black cockerel were added.

These devilish ingredients were mixed with clay from a river bed and water from a waterfall on which the moonlight shone, then moulded into the form of a witch-puppet. Its eyes were berries from the ivy in the churchyard.

When her sinister deed was nearly done, the gipsy breathed upon the image, all the while muttering strange spells. She passed the doll through the night air, through the flames of her wood fire and through the ripples of the mountain stream.

The screech of her laughter echoed from the mountain-side as she took a splinter from a broken looking glass and thrust it into the doll's chest.

Far away in the lamplight of his stone house, so the story goes, Old Trickitt cried out as he felt a sudden pain in his heart, and fell dead upon the hearth.

A Fairy Brew

There was once an old widow who lived with her son, Willie John, in a cottage near the north coast of Gower. Early one morning she was in her garden feeding the chickens when a strange thing happened. Above the crowing of the cocks and the clucking of the hens she heard a voice calling to her.

'Old lady,' she heard the voice say, 'favour us with a kindness.'

She looked about her and saw several of the Verry Volk standing there in the sunlight beside a bed of primroses. They had come to her garden from the fairy knoll on the heath.

'What is it you want of me?' the widow asked.

The Fairy Folk explained that they were rewarding the villagers for their kindly deeds and measuring little bags of gold dust, one for each family who had won their friendship.

'It is not easy to separate the dust from the tiny nuggets,' they sighed. 'Pray, lend us your sieve to make our task less tedious.'

They pointed to the sieve with which the widow's son strained the hops to flavour his home-brewed ale.

'To be sure, you're quite welcome,' the old woman said.

She took the sieve from its nail on the wall and gave it to the Fairy Folk who wheeled it along the garden path and across the heath.

'You're quite welcome,' she called after them, for she certainly had no wish to offend the Verry Volk.

Later that night, when the lamp was lit and she was busy at her sewing, there came a faint tapping on the door. There was no-one standing in the doorway when she lifted the latch. There was nothing but the old sieve leaning against the wall.

The spring passed and summer drew on, with much thirsty work to do in the fields. Before long the ale cask was nearly empty. So, one Sunday after chapel, the widow's son strained the hops to replenish his stock, for there was nothing he liked better than a drink of ale when his day's toil was done.

The fresh brew was unusually potent, and it was noticed that after just a draught or two of the home-made beverage he became strangely intoxicated. There was a sparkle in his eyes and he felt an

inclination to dance around the floor as though someone were plucking a merry tune on the harp and the music held him entranced. This odd recital seemed to become a regular occurrence, for each evening at sundown, when supper was over and a mug or two of ale had been consumed, there he was dancing around the table and before the hearth without a worldly care. And all the while the widow busied herself with her sewing, for she heard only the wind sighing in the chimney and the distant cry of an owl.

'This is the strongest ale I've ever brewed,' he said to her one night as he filled his mug from the cask.

Before that summer was over, Willie John's ale was the talk of North Gower. At harvest time the local taverns were almost deserted for, when their day's reaping was done, farmers and their sons from Cheriton and Llangennith came by horse and cart to Willie John's cottage in Llanmadoc to taste his special brew. Night after night the lamp glowed in the window. From sunset until the first light of dawn showed, the sound of raucous voices and dancing feet drifted across the heath. Mysteriously, no matter how often the jugs were refilled, like the well at the bottom of the garden, the cask remained full. Through autumn and the chill nights of winter, folk from miles around drank their fill from the everlasting cask of ale. And from the first draught each was strangely intoxicated and became bewitched by a strange music. Once, twirling a lively reel, they were all lured along the moonlit garden toward the fairy knoll on the heath.

These nights of merry-making came to an abrupt end before the winter was over. It so happened that one day, while sitting in her rocking chair reminiscing over the events of past months, the old widow recalled how the Verry Volk had come to ask a favour and had returned to the cottage after nightfall.

'It all began that moonlit night when they came knocking at the door,' she told her son. 'It's likely they put a spell on the sieve when they brought it back. I do declare, that sieve is bewitched!'

And so it came about that the secret was revealed and the spell was broken, for that was the way with the Fairy Folk. That very night the cask ran dry. But, among the cobwebs in the corner where it stood, the old widow came upon a little bag of gold dust – enough to buy the seed to grow their corn, to keep them fed for the rest of their days.

Old Moll

No-one can say for sure where Old Moll lived, or when. It is said that she lived like a hermit in a shack among the bracken on Fairwood Common. Others say that she combed the beaches near Brandy Cove and slept at night in a cave beneath the heather on the cliff-top. Some claim that she roamed from place to place, begging and stealing and telling fortunes for pennies. But wherever she spent her days she was always alone, for she was too ill-tempered and sharp-tongued to make friends with ordinary folk.

Strange tales of Old Moll spread from village to village. Wherever she wandered, misfortune befell the inhabitants. Cattle became lean and sickly, crops withered in the fields, and once a child who mocked at her wizened face was mysteriously plagued with fearful nightmares.

Before long everyone was convinced that she was a witch and whenever she came in sight the villagers drove her off with jeers and stones. Many a time she would skulk away muttering oaths at her pursuers.

But although she was old and bent no-one could catch her because, when she was chased, she changed herself into a hare and escaped capture with her speed and cunning.

It was well known in those days that wearing a ring or a brooch of silver would drive away the evil of witchcraft, so the villagers decided to rid themselves forever of Old Moll and her dark spells. Buttons and coins of silver were collected and taken to the local blacksmith's where they were forged into bullets.

Then one evening the hunched figure of Old Moll was seen gathering firewood on the edge of a copse. The villagers gave chase, but instantly she changed into a hare and went fleeting through the trees.

Alas, a silver bullet found its mark and the animal was wounded in the leg. It let out a pitiful animal cry and for a while lay writhing in the undergrowth.

While the villagers were searching in the copse the hare managed to crawl away and hide. Bloodstains were seen on the ground, but no-one found Old Moll because now she was more than 100 paces away crouching in the bracken. She was breathing quickly and her cloak was all about her.

It was almost dark when she came from her hiding place. She was never again seen on Fairwood Common nor on the beaches to the south. But that was not the last folk heard of Old Moll. It is said that many times she was seen wandering alone among the hills and cwms of Glamorgan. And wherever she went she walked with a limp and carried a stick to help her along.

The Legend of Frenni Fach

Lying to the east of the Preseli Mountains are the hills of Frenni Fach and Frenni Fawr, a great expanse of high moorland and rough pasture which has changed little over the past 200 years. If ever you wander there among the hills on a balmy summer day, you will hear the plaintive bleat of sheep and the trill of the skylark's song.

It was on such a day long ago that a shepherd boy roamed the slopes of Frenni Fach, tending his father's flock. Wisps of cirrus fanned out over the hilltop and the sun was warm on his back. After trudging along for a mile or more he came to a mountain brook, where he paused for a while to drink from the sparkling water.

While he rested there, the faint sound of music came from a hillside nearby. At first he thought it was the brook murmuring on its way, but then, unmistakably, he heard the strains of a harp. He followed the sound along the craggy banks until he came to a knoll strewn with bracken.

Here, for the first time in his life, he set eyes on the Tylwyth Teg (Fairy Folk). They were dancing happily in a fairy ring. Fearing that he would frighten them away, he edged forward stealthily until he lay among the bracken just a few paces away. They were elegantly dressed in stockings and cloaks of scarlet and blue, with pixie hats as bright as sunlight.

Delicately they twirled and reeled, always careful to stay within the fairy ring. After a while, they caught sight of the shepherd boy and beckoned him to join in their dance. He stepped inside the ring and instantly the haunting music charmed away all worldly cares. A luxuriant garden appeared before him, and a path leading to a magnificent palace glistened white in the sunshine.

'This shall be your home, gentle shepherd,' the Fairy Folk told him. 'Stay here forever among your new friends of the Other World. This prince's palace is yours. But beware – the brook that flows through the garden measures another time and is not of our world.'

The boy gasped at the wonder of it all.

And there, in his strange new surroundings, the shepherd boy lived like a prince for a long while. Weeks passed, but not once did he think of his home on the shoulder of Frenni Fach. The palace garden changed from season to season; the green of summer, the gold of autumn, and drooping boughs capped with snow.

Then one day while he was walking beside the brook he remembered the Fairy Folk's warning, and began to wonder about the other world to which the brook belonged, and the different time it measured. He kneeled on the bank and let the water trickle through his hands. It sparkled in the sunshine.

The moment the first drop touched his lips all the birds were silent. Then the garden and the palace melted away into the blue sky, and he found himself kneeling beside the brook on Frenni Fach. On the hills around him the sheep were grazing peacefully as he had left them.

It was dusk when he arrived at his home on the eastern slopes of the hill, and the farmhouse was hidden among the long shadows. He

93

thought it strange that although he had been away for two summers or more, no-one ran to greet him. His folks were about their evening tasks as usual. They smiled as he crossed the threshold as though he had been away for but a day.

In the days that followed, the shepherd boy looked sadly round the hills for signs of the Tylwyth Teg and their magic fairy ring. But although he searched from Frenni Fach to the mists of the Preseli Mountains, they were never seen again.

Ghost Island

Sometimes on a clear day, folk who know the legend of Ghost Island scan the horizon off the coast of Pembrokeshire. But they see only the shimmering waters of St Brides Bay and a distant haze, for the mysterious isle has not been seen for more than 200 years.

One June morning in the 18th century some fishermen put out to sea. Their vessel left the shore to the south of St Davids and slid silently through the mist. They had sailed only a short distance from land when the mist broke and golden rays of sunlight shone down upon an uncharted island which appeared before them. Barely two miles from east to west, it was fringed with white sand and its verdant hills stood against the sky. The crew gazed over the bows, hardly able to believe their eyes.

A while later they rowed ashore to explore the island, for although they had sailed around the coast of Pembrokeshire for many a year not a man aboard had set eyes on it before.

As they set foot on the beach they looked warily toward the caves where the sound of the waves echoed like a thousand voices whispering to them.

The island was deserted, and at length they returned to their vessel and sailed away. The sun dispersed the mist and then, strange to say, the island vanished too. Like a mirage the white sands and the rolling hills disappeared.

The legend of Ghost Island became well known throughout the county of Pembrokeshire, and this 'Green Isle of the Sea' aroused much interest.

Many summers passed. Then one day Gruffydd ab Einon (Griffith son of Einon), a native of St Davids, was visiting a grave in the churchyard when once again the island appeared a short distance out at sea. He hurried to the beach, but before he had left the shore the island was nowhere to be seen.

This strange revelation happened time and again. Whenever Gruffydd looked out to sea from the churchyard at St Davids the island appeared off-shore, only to vanish again before he had time to put to sea.

Now there lived at that time in the county of Pembrokeshire a

'Knowing One' – an old woman whom many believed was a witch. So one day Gruffydd called at her stone hut on the hillside. If anyone knew the secret of the ghostly island it would be she.

The stout door creaked as she let him in. As she listened to Gruffydd's story she stirred the fire and watched the flames flicker in the chimney. After a while she shuffled close, with her stick tap-tapping on the floor.

'You are a favoured one,' she said at length. 'Few mortals set eyes on the home of Rhys the Deep, patriarch of the Fairy Folk.'

'A ghost island!' Gruffydd declared. 'It appears in the sunlight and then vanishes beneath the sea.'

The old hag chuckled and shook her head. 'Strange herbs grow on the hillside,' she explained. 'They grow there and nowhere else, so the island cannot be seen – except from the turf of St Davids churchyard, for the herbs are believed to grow there also.'

He gave the old woman a silver coin and went on his way.

The next morning at first light Gruffydd ab Einon stood among the gravestones at St Davids churchyard looking out to sea. Then, beneath the early rays of sunlight, the Green Isle appeared. As usual he put to sea, but this time he took with him the turf on which he had been standing.

As he rowed out into St Brides Bay he looked over his shoulder, and all the while the island remained in sight. Before long he was pulling his boat ashore on the white sands. He wandered toward the caves where he received a friendly welcome from the Fairy Folk.

Now that the secret was known, he visited the spectral isle on many occasions. He was shown their treasures and watched them dance to the haunting music which echoed through the caverns beneath the hills.

As the years passed, Gruffydd spent more and more time in the kingdom of Rhys the Deep. Then one evening he set off on his usual journey and was never seen again. Some say he was lost at sea, others that he tired of worldly cares and spent the rest of his life on the Green Isle.

Since that time long ago the island has never again appeared. But many folk believe that it lies there still, invisible in the grey of the mist and sea. It is thought that sometimes the island's inhabitants visit the markets on the mainland, for strange people have been seen in the coastal towns from Milford Haven and Pembroke Dock in the south to Fishguard in the north: even as far inland as Haverfordwest. And their presence has been known there since early in the 19th century – long before the days of tourists.

Lady of the Lake

The Black Mountain range straddles the old counties of Brecknock and Carmarthenshire. On its western flank, where sometimes buzzards are seen circling overhead, stands Mynydd Du (The Black Mountain) itself, 1,000 feet above sea level. From its summit cliffs fall 500 feet into the still, clear water of Llyn-y-Fan Fach.

Here, at the farm Blaensawdde in Llanddeusant which lies in the shire of Carmarthen, there once lived a young peasant called Rhiwallon. His father and brothers had been killed while fighting the Normans when they came to conquer Wales, so now he was left alone with his widowed mother. Together they worked hard for a living on their small mountain farm.

One day Rhiwallon drove his cows up the mountainside, and there in the warm sunshine he fell asleep beside the lake. When he awoke and looked about him he could hardly believe his eyes, for on the surface of the water stood the fairest maiden he had seen in all his life. Her eyes were as blue as the summer sky and her hair as golden as sunlight. He called to her, and a moment later she disappeared beneath the surface. There was no ripple on the water; no sound but the fast beating of his heart. He waited beside the lake until the lowing of the cattle told him it was time to make his way home. But she did not reappear.

All night long he lay awake, thinking about the Lady of the Lake.

The following morning, soon after sunrise, he drove his cattle to the hillside and stood beside the lake watching and waiting. At last he saw her again, standing upon the water just as before. He called to her and she smiled.

'Lady of the Lake,' he said boldly. 'There is nothing I would not give if only you will leave your under-water world and live with me.'

But as he spoke the image grew faint and then vanished.

Several days passed before he saw her again. Each morning he drove his cattle to the lakeside, and at dusk he trudged sadly down the mountain. Then one evening as he was about to make his way home he took one last glance over his shoulder and saw her resting on a rock beside the lake. Happily he ran to her and stood there admiring her beauty.

'Lady of the Lake,' he said solemnly, 'unless you love me as I love

you I would rather drown in your world than be alone in mine.'

For a moment her blue eyes twinkled. Then she plunged into the waters of Llyn-y-Fan Fach, leaving the slanting rays of sunlight dancing on the surface.

In a little while she reappeared, and at her side was a tall, white-haired gentleman in a mantle of silk. He gave his daughter's hand to Rhiwallon and in a deep resonant voice he said, 'Young mortal, if your heart is kind and true she will live with you until the end of your days.'

Then, seeing Rhiwallon's eyes light up with joy, he raised his hand and warned, 'In our world we live in peace and think only of others. There is never a word uttered in reproach or anger. So if, during your wedded life, you should three times lay hand on her other than in love and tenderness, you shall lose her forever.'

Then he summoned from the depths of the lake a drove of cattle, sheep, goats, horses and oxen. They emerged from the water under a fountain of silvery spray, with a neighing and a braying and a lowing.

When all their farewells were said and the shadows lengthened, Rhiwallon and the Lady of the Lake made their way down the mountain path, and her dowry trailed behind them.

That springtime they were married and made their home at a farm near the village of Myddfai. Happily the years tumbled along and they were blessed with fine sons and daughters. And because their life together was filled with joy, Rhiwallon was always mindful of the old man's warning. He was never unkind nor did he once lay hand on his wife other than in love and tenderness.

Then one summer morning he was harnessing the horse and carriage in readiness for their journey to the church at Myddfai where they were to attend a christening. But all the while his wife was sad, for she foresaw events unknown to other folk.

'The child will see no more than five birthdays,' she said with a sigh.

Rhiwallon was impatient. 'Come along,' he reproached, 'or we shall be late.' And he tapped her lightly on the shoulder to hurry her along.

His wife looked at him sadly. 'You have forgotten my father's warning never to lay hand on me reproachfully.'

Years passed by, and Rhiwallon had again almost forgotten the vow he made so long ago on the banks of Llyn-y-Fan Fach. Then one evening they were attending a wedding feast at a nearby village. There was much laughter and merriment on this happy occasion, but Rhiwallon was surprised to see his wife weeping quietly.

'Come now,' he chided, tapping her arm gently. 'This is a time for joy not tears.'

'You forget that I foresee what is unknown to others,' his wife replied. 'How can I be gay when I know the sorrow that lies before them.'

Then, realising that for the second time Rhiwallon's vow had been broken, they looked anxiously at one another.

Because their devotion to their children and their love for each other was as precious as ever, they had no wish to be parted. So from that day onward Rhiwallon took care that no word of reproach escaped his lips.

The years drew on, each one happier than the last. Then one day they went to the churchyard at Myddfai where they gathered around the grave of an old friend. All was black and tearful. But standing there among the mourners, Rhiwallon's wife was smiling happily. Rhiwallon nudged her gently, laying his hand upon her.

'Why should you smile at this time of grief?' he asked in an angry whisper.

'I smile because our friend is now free of worldly cares,' she replied.

A moment later, Rhiwallon saw her eyes fill with tears, for now he had broken his vow for the third and last time. Then the silver in her hair turned to gold and she became again the fair maiden of Llyn-y-Fan Fach.

'Farewell, Rhiwallon,' she sighed, and made her way to their farm at Esgair Llaethdy near the village of Myddfai. There she called together all her animals – those that had come out of the lake so long ago and all their progeny. Cattle came from the fields and byres; oxen plodded to her, dragging their plough behind them; sheep with their lambs ran bleating to her from the folds and pastures; goats came skipping from the copses and leaping from the rocks; white stallions with flowing manes whinnied about her.

A host of creatures thronged the mountain path. At their head was the black bull of Esgair Llaethdy, with crumpled horns and snorting nostrils, and led by the Lady of the Lake.

Long shadows lay across the hills when they reached the banks of Llyn-y-Fan Fach. Before the moon was bright in the sky the waters had closed over them, leaving only the furrow torn by the plough and hoofprints on the dusty path.

Time and again Rhiwallon lingered there, but never again did he see his Lady of the Lake.

And here the legend of Llyn-y-Fan Fach might have ended, for when the fair maiden returned to the Otherworld, nothing more was heard of Rhiwallon. But whenever his sons were in the mountains they wandered around the lake hoping to see their mother reappear on the sun-flecked water.

Then one morning, as the eldest son was making his way to the pastureland, he heard a voice calling to him. And there she was like a veil of mist above the water.

'My son,' he heard her say, 'there is work for you to do in your

101

world – to heal the sick and comfort the helpless: to be a great physician.'

'If only I had the knowledge,' her son replied.

The voice echoed from the cliffs of Mynydd Du. She told her son how she would be his guide and teacher.

And so it came about that Rhiwallon's sons devoted their lives to the arts of medicine. The spirit of the lake led them to places where rare herbs grew, and taught them how to brew healing potions. They became the most skilled healers of the sick in Wales and their fame spread all over Britain. To this day they are known as Meddygon Myddfai (the Physicians of Myddfai).*

For more than 800 years their skill was preserved from generation to generation. The last known of these magical healers was Sir John Williams who was physician to Queen Victoria. He died in 1920.

Nowadays Llyn-y-Fan Fach, a silvery mirror hidden in the mountains, is as quiet and enchanting as ever. Sometimes, when the wind blows' over Mynydd Du, it seems that a voice whispers across the lake. And if you were to search carefully along the south bank you would find deep furrows, buried now beneath the heather. They run to the edge of the water, as though a long time ago the blades of a plough had torn through the earth.

* The knowledge of the Meddygon Myddfai was written down in a book which can be read today. The *Physicians of Myddfai* contains many remedies which seem strange in the 20th century.

A light dinner and less supper, sound sleep and a long life.

If thou desirest to die, eat cabbage in August.

Take the gall of a cat and hen's fat, mixing them together. Put this on your eyes, and you will see things which are invisible to others.

Bewitched

Sally-Anne lived with her grandmother at Trefelyn, a hamlet close to the shores of Cardigan Bay. No-one came to visit them in their cottage in the valley, for it was generally believed that the old woman was a witch and the neighbours were afraid of her. As for Sally-Anne, she was a quiet girl, almost 16-years-old, with dark hair and sad, brown eyes.

Every morning she walked across the hills to Mathry where she worked on a farm just outside the village. There she helped with the housework and tended the animals. She fed the chickens, led the cows to pasture, and in springtime when the sheep were brought down from the hills she would wander off to watch the lambs frisking in the lowland meadows. She was never more contented than when she was alone with the animals, for she loved them all. Sometimes she would linger in the meadows for hour after hour while the farmer's wife searched for her everywhere.

'Sally-Anne!' she would call impatiently through the stalls of the byre and around the barn. 'Where on earth can she be?'

But Sally-Anne was never to be found. She was always away on the hills or in the meadows. Time and again the washing and cleaning were left undone while she strayed far from the farmhouse. On many occasions the farmer and his wife were obliged to reproach her sternly and remind her of her duties. But she would only frown and explain how the animals would fret if she were not there to care for them. She took little notice of their warning, so one day late on in the spring the farmer called her from the meadow and sent her home to her grandmother.

'And don't ever come back again!' he said angrily as the tears welled up in her eyes.

Dejectedly, Sally-Anne made her way over the hills to Trefelyn. When she told her grandmother what had happened she threw up her arms in despair, for the butter and eggs and small wages which the girl brought home was all they had to live on. For the rest of the day the old woman sat in her rocking chair stroking her sleek black cat. Until long after dark she sat there muttering to herself.

The following morning when the farmer went to the byre he found

103

the bull kicking and snorting, its hoofs tearing the earth floor of the stall. The cows, too, were ill-tempered, lowing and tugging at their chains. With feathers ruffled, the cocks fought in the coop and the hens had not laid. In the meadows the sheep were restive and many of the lambs had followed the ewes into the hills.

The farmer was puzzled to see his animals behaving so, for nothing as unusual had happened before. And when, throughout the next day, nothing he did would console them he became alarmed.

'A strange spell has come over them!' he said to his wife.

That evening, in their cottage across the hills, Sally-Anne and her grandmother sat together in the lamplight. The old woman was rocking to and fro and she chuckled to herself. 'Don't fret, child,' she said. 'As likely as not you'll soon hear a knocking at the door and you'll be back with your animals on the farm before the week is out.'

GHOSTS AND SUCH

The White Lady

An old manor house once stood in the village of Bishopston on the Gower Peninsula. It was the home of the local rector whose wife had been dead many a year. As far as is known he had no children and he lived there alone in retirement.

One night on his way to bed he paused suddenly in the hall, unable to believe his eyes, for there appeared before him the figure of a lady dressed all in white. She moved silently along the corridor, ascended the stairs, then disappeared in the shadows.

Since nothing quite as odd had happened to him before, he decided that a shaft of moonlight had come slanting through the window and had played tricks with his imagination. But the next night, and many more times that summer, the figure of the White Lady materialised from nowhere in the rooms of the manor. Each time he saw her she became more real and more frightful than the time before. On the first occasion she appeared just as a misty shape, but now her sallow complexion and burning eyes were clearly visible. After a while her presence was accompanied by a most terrifying noise. It was like the murmur of a heart-beat which grew loud and louder still until it echoed through the house. At the same time the furniture began to tremble and curtains swayed from side to side.

Each time the old man saw the eerie shape and heard the dreaded sound he became more and more afraid until at last he could stand it no longer. So at the first sound of the ghost's approach he would flee from the house and stumble across the common. There he would stay until the spectre had gone, and even then it took some time for him to summon enough courage to venture back indoors.

On several occasions villagers from the neighbouring cottages returned to the manor with him. But each time the house was still, and if the truth were known, they suspected that the old man had become eccentric in his old age.

The rector lived in fear of nightfall, until one evening a gipsy woman called at the house, peddling her rush mats and coloured ribbon. When the door opened she looked at the rector standing there, then beyond him into the dusky hallway. Fear showed in her eyes. She clutched her basket in her arms and stepped back from the threshold.

'Ysbrydion ... Ysbrydion,' (ghosts) she muttered, for she sensed an evil presence in the house.

The old man followed her into the garden, knowing that gipsies had a strange understanding of spirits and their haunting ways. It was there that he learned an old gipsy remedy with which he might overcome the ghost. The White Lady, she told him, must be put to the test of the bell and candle.

Not long afterwards, this peculiar test was arranged. From Bishopston and other villages nearby, the rector gathered together 12 men of the church. After dark they came to the manor house and stood around the kitchen table upon which 12 candles and 12 handbells were placed.

According to the gipsy's story, haunting spirits always seek darkness and are angered by the peal of bells. So when the hour of midnight approached, candles were to be lit and the handbells rung. It was said that the ghost would brave the noise of the bells and attempt to blow out the lights which offended her. If every flame was extinguished before the 12th stroke of the clock, then the ghost could never be driven away and the house would remain forever haunted. But if just one flame still burned, then the ghost would be defeated and her earthly conquerors must give her some task to perform which would keep her away for all time.

Midnight came. Then weird sounds were heard. Heart-beats grew loud like peals of thunder. Furniture trembled. Curtains rustled as though a wind had stirred them. The sounds which heralded the White Lady's approach tempted the clerics to flee, but they drew courage from one another.

The clock began to strike. A flowing, white gown and the fiery eyes of the ghost appeared. In a rage she blew out the first candle. But as the 12 godly men chanted aloud their prayers and rang the handbells, the ghost became alarmed and confused. Meanwhile the clock struck on, and she rushed among them in great distress, feverishly blowing over their shoulders.

But at the last stroke of midnight candlelight still flickered on their faces. The poor lady stood sadly in a corner awaiting their judgement.

Then the clerics pronounced their sentence. She was banished from the house and sent to a point below high water in Caswell Bay. There she was to build a castle of sand which would withstand the force of the waves during the ebb and flow of the tide.

The White Lady was never again seen or heard in the village of Bishopston. But if ever you overlook the beach at Caswell you will see a peculiar stirring of the sand in the middle of the bay. Some say it is where an inland stream meets the sea. But others know that a ghost is busily digging there. They know, too, that it is not a whisper of wind that comes from Caswell Valley, but the sound of the White Lady rushing around in a vain attempt to stop the cruel tide washing away her sand castle.

A Visitor at Castlebythe

There are not many places in the south-west corner of Wales more remote than the little hamlet of Castlebythe, surrounded by rolling heath, with Castlebythe Mountain to the north, strewn with ancient ruins and burial mounds. Nowadays, with the main roads passing by several miles away, the hamlet has few visitors. 100 years ago, with no mechanised transport and primitive roadways, it was just a desolate expanse of moorland sheltering a number of lonely farmhouses.

However, one visitor to Castlebythe has been remembered for many a year, and as long as tales are told around the hearth this visitor is never likely to be forgotten. No-one knows where this uninvited guest came from, nor the reason for his presence there. Yet, for several evenings in the winter of 1874, mystery and fear lingered at an old farmhouse on the hillside.

It all began one night when the family were sitting around the simne fawr (big chimney). There was a bright moon and a wind sighed under the eaves. No footsteps were heard, but for some unknown reason the dog's hackles rose and he skirted the room, growling and baring his teeth. A lamp standing on the table began to flicker. Then, by some invisible presence, it was flung against the wall with a startling crash, leaving only the flames in the grate to light the room. A moment later, smoke came billowing from the fireplace while first the window rattled and then the whole house began to tremble. The farmer and his wife were seized with fright at such an uncanny occurrence.

After a little while the smoke cleared and the house was still. That night the inhabitants of the farmhouse slept fitfully in their beds.

The next day passed uneventfully, but when evening came a strange rattling noise was heard coming from an outhouse across the yard. Cattle lowed in the byre and the horses whinnied restively in the stables. From the doorway the dog barked and snarled and then came slinking under the kitchen table. When, at length, the farmer ventured into the outhouse the light of his lantern fell on an extraordinary sight. A revolving butter churn was turning end over end with a hollow clatter and clang. A large stone was found inside,

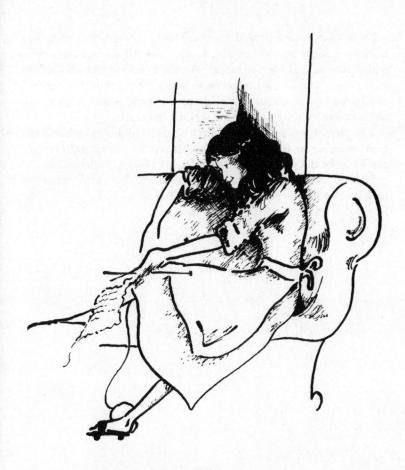

but who had placed it there, and what mysterious force turned the churn over and over, no-one ever knew.

The following evening, not long after nightfall, the folk at the farmhouse had finished their supper and were seated as usual around the simne fawr. Uneasily their eyes searched the shadows as they watched and listened for the ghostly visitor to return.

An hour passed by, and another. Then the lamp flickered and dimmed, and someone was heard in a dark corner of the room. Nothing was seen as the sound of a voice – low and murmuring – moved toward the fireplace. But no-one could distinguish the words. It lingered for a while by the small window, and then grew faint as it passed outside in the direction of the outhouse.

More lamps were lit and candles placed around. Everyone was wide-eyed with fear. Then the farmer noticed something which, oddly, no-one had noticed before. A young servant girl who helped in the dairy was sitting on the settle under the window. She seemed unaffected by the ghostly presence at the farmhouse, for even now she sat there knitting quietly and smiling to herself.

The farmer was angry. Brusquely he ordered her to bed, and the next morning at first light she was taken by horse and carriage across the bridge over the Afon Angof to her home in Puncheston.

Folk say that when the servant girl left Castlebythe the visitor left with her, for he was never seen nor heard again.

Someone on the Stairs

It was in 1897 when strange happenings began at Clyneway Cottage. One evening in summer a gardener who was living there at the time was on his way home from work when he heard his young daughter calling to someone in the branches of a tree.

'Wendy ... Wendy ...' she was calling over and over again. 'I know you're hiding there.'

But her father saw no-one hiding in the branches. What was more surprising, Wendy – who wasn't really there at all – then climbed down from the tree and chased his daughter across the lawn. There they played together for some time. But it was only the footprints of his daughter Molly which appeared on the grass.

When their playing was over, Molly began to sing to herself. It was then that her father became alarmed, for he fancied he heard another faraway voice singing with her. Standing there in the evening light, he felt strangely ill at ease.

It was getting dark when Molly went to bed. As she lay on the pillow with her rag doll clutched in her arms, her father said to her, 'Cariad,' (darling) 'who is Wendy?'

'I don't know,' Molly replied. 'She came to me one day in the garden. Now we play together always. Sometimes she calls to me before I'm awake.'

Her father blew out the candle at her bedside and kissed her forehead.

In the days that followed, Molly spent most of her time out in the sunshine. Each day she played with Wendy – the little girl who wasn't there. They hid from each other among the rhododendron bushes, and together they lay on the low stone bridge which crossed the stream beside the cottage, looking at the reflections in the water. And when the sun had gone, they walked together in the shadows. It was always at this old bridge where Molly waved goodbye to her friend. If Wendy was a ghost she haunted only the garden and the banks of the stream, for she never came into the cottage. Not until one night, late in the summer.

On that particular night, Molly's father was awakened by an unusual sound. He heard a voice outside his bedroom door. He lit

the candle and went to the top of the stairs. His wife did not stir, and a peep into Molly's room showed him that she, too, was fast asleep. But there was only darkness on the stairway.

The next night it happened again. The voice of a child crying was heard in the cottage. This time the gardener and his wife were awakened. They went out to the landing and looked over the banister. Moonlight was coming through the window and making strange shadows on the stairs. But no-one was standing there, and the voice of someone weeping sadly was there all the time.

After a while, a door opened behind them and Molly was standing in the doorway.

'I dreamt that Wendy was calling me,' she said, rubbing her eyes sleepily. 'But it wasn't a dream. She is really here!'

She took the candle from her father, and step by step she walked down into the shadows. The crying stopped.

'She's going far away,' she went on, as she descended the stairs, 'and she's come to say goodbye.'

For a while, Molly stood there in the candlelight, sometimes listening, sometimes whispering to a ghostly presence on the stairs. Eventually, she came back up to the landing and there were tears in her eyes. She turned and called out to the shadows, 'Goodbye, Wendy.'

And on that summer night there was, just for a moment, a chill in the cottage, as if the door had opened and a breeze had blown in from the garden.

Is Anyone There?

Throughout Wales there are countless tales of ghosts who haunt the scene of earthly tragedy. There is y ladi wen (the white lady) who jealously guards a buried treasure within the walls of Ogmore Castle; the grey lady who crosses the bridge beneath the towers of Cardiff Castle where her lover was once imprisoned; a forlorn woman, searching the banks of the Taff for her lost child; a hideous hag clad all in green, screaming about the slanting tower at Caerphilly; the black-robed monk of Caldy Island ... Almost every spectre wails and moans or walks in silent sorrow. But not all ghosts are of grim humour reliving a tale of woe.

(1) The house stood at the edge of the village where the road bent and wandered off over the shoulder of the hill. Its walls were grey and on the north side moss clung all about it. There were no curtains behind the window panes, no smoke in the chimney. The house was empty.

One fine morning, long ago, a woman from the village set off along the road for a farm in the hills. As she passed by the deserted house she was attracted by a most unusual sound. From somewhere within the empty rooms there came the voice of a child singing an old Welsh lullaby. It was a sweet, clear voice that came tumbling out into the sunshine.

For a while the woman listened. Then, opening the gate, she picked her way along the crazy path, lifted the latch and went inside.

'Is anyone there?' she called into the dusky hall.

She was sure it was the voice of a little girl that went on singing happily, 'Breichiau mam sy'n dyn am danat.' (Mother's arms are folding round you.)

It was coming from a room above. A faded clock-shape showed on the paper in the hall, and into the front room sunlight came streaming. The woman called again, but no-one answered her. So she climbed the stairs. The rooms were bare and only her steps were printed on the dusty floors. Although she searched high and low, in hidden alcoves and dark cupboards, there was no-one to be seen.

She was very puzzled when she left the house and went on her way. Even as she climbed the shoulder of the hill the faint sound of singing could still be heard.

It was long past sunset when she was returning to the village. As she hurried round the bend in the road she saw the house standing dark against the sky. No lights burned in the windows and all was silent beyond the open gate.

(2) Long ago there was a young man who lived to the north of Pendine, a village on the coast of Carmarthen. He had golden hair and eyes that sparkled. To all the village folk he was known as Crythor,* for whenever they held a Noson Lawen (Merry Evening) he played jolly tunes on his fiddle until the villagers were too weary to dance any longer.

One summer evening when the merry making was over he set off toward his cottage among the hills. On the way he came upon a band of Tylwyth Teg (Fairy Folk) dressed all in scarlet and green

---

*Crythor was the name given to one who played the old Welsh stringed instrument, the crwth, similar to the violin.

115

and gathered in a wooded dell. They stood there boldly as he approached.

'Crythor, play us a tune on your fiddle,' said one with a mischievous smile. 'Make music so that we can dance.'

So the young man, not wishing to offend the fairy folk, played his fiddle while they leapt and twirled about him in the moonlight.

At length they tired of dancing, and before the last of their band had disappeared into the shadows she turned to the fiddler and said, 'Remember, Crythor, that under the hills not far away is a cave without an end. There your fiddle will turn to gold and learn the music of the fairy folk.'

All his life the young man had been poor, so the promise of gold made his heart beat fast. And the haunting melodies of the Tylwyth Teg were the wonder of everyone. So in the days that followed he searched through the caves on the hillside. Autumn drew on, but though he looked in every nook and cranny neither he nor anyone else could solve the riddle of the cave without an end.

Then one morning when the snow lay heavy on the hills he set off from his cottage to continue his quest for the elusive cave. At each entrance he listened and called into the darkness. 'Is anyone there?' Then he would venture inside and fiddle the tune he had played in the fairy dell. But no-one answered him, and each time the rocky pathway under the hill came to an end. He called and fiddled among the hills as he had done each day through summer and autumn. But before nightfall he had vanished and was never seen again.

Some folk say he was lost in the snow drifts. Others claim that if ever you take the footpath through the hills north of Pendine, passing by tumulus and chambered cairns of long ago, you will hear strange music echoing through an underground cavern, for there the ghost of Crythor with a fiddle of gold plays the music of the Tylwyth Teg.

Phantom of Crack Hill

If you ever travel from Bridgend on the main road to Cardiff you will pass over the Ewenny bridge and through the hamlet of Brocastle. Then you will come to a stretch of highway known as Crack Hill, where the road climbs over featureless moorland for a distance of a mile or so and then continues eastward.

At the end of the 19th century Crack Hill was an old Roman road edged with bracken and rough pasture-land behind the dry-stone walls. Near the bottom of the hill stood a milestone, recording the five miles to Cowbridge. But at night it was either lost in the darkness or silhouetted in the moonlight like a stone marking a lonely grave. It was a desolate spot, and to the superstitious folk thereabouts it was known as a favourite haunt of the Devil.

Late one summer's evening a traveller who lived at Pentremeyrick was making his way home from Bridgend. Black clouds were

building up on the horizon and an occasional rumble of thunder was heard in the south. He dug his heels into the horse's flanks and it broke into a gentle trot, soon reaching the lower slope of Crack Hill.

For a while only the clip-clop of the horse's hoofs disturbed the silence. But then, faintly at first, the traveller heard the sound of another horse approaching from some distance away. He turned in the saddle, but the road was deserted. Presently he heard the sound again, distinctly now, as though a rider passed close by and went galloping on up the hill. The traveller's horse reared.

'Whoa, fy merch i,' (Steady, girl) he said as her hoofs tore into the dirt road.

Back and forth along Crack Hill went the phantom rider. Galloping hoofs were clearly audible, waxing and waning like the peals of thunder overhead. But there was neither horse nor rider to be seen. Then once, as the ghostly sound passed close by, the traveller felt something clutching at his shoulders, as though someone had leapt into the saddle behind him. Again his horse shied, throwing him to the ground; and as it ran off up the hill the traveller scrambled to his feet, with something still clung fast about his shoulders. Terrified, he swung around, clawing at his back. But the awesome burden would not release its hold on him. So he lumbered on up the hill, struggling against the weight which bore him down and crying out in fright.

When he was near the top a bolt of lightning lit up the road. And then, just as suddenly as it had come upon him, whatever clung to his shoulders set him free. For the last time galloping hoofs were heard nearby, as though the phantom steed had returned for its rider. After a moment or two they were heard no more.

The Cellar

The tavern stood next to a row of cottages beside a road which led into the suburbs of Swansea. To the north lay a range of hills, and the Tawe flowed south through the valley. It was a bleak, old house. In winter the east wind whined under the gable, and even on a summer's day the trees about the garden kept the house in shadow.

Many an evening, when the ale flowed freely, there was a glow in the windows and the rooms rang with the sounds of laughter and raucous song. But often, when the lights went out and the night wore on, a haunting sound came to disturb the silence.

This ghostly presence was first discovered more than 100 years ago. It so happened that one night after the tavern's shutters were fastened and the doors bolted, the landlord was alone in a room downstairs. He was putting out the fires before retiring to bed when he heard the faint sounds of someone weeping. He unlocked a door which led to the cellar, for that was where the voice seemed to come from. Then he stood above the flight of stone steps, his lantern searching out the dark corners below. He leaned over the banisters, and from somewhere in the shadowy rooms beneath the steps there came a sobbing and a sighing; a soft voice like that of a child. This went on for a long while – weeping, minutes of silence, and then the pitiful sounds would come again. The landlord peered down over the banister and the lantern trembled in his hand.

In the years that followed, so the story goes, the haunting voice was heard in the cellar of the tavern time and again. It is said that many different landlords came and went, but the ghost remained until the winter of 1937, when the tavern was destroyed by fire.

No-one ever knew why a ghost came to haunt the tavern, and there is no record of any sinister happening there. But recently some 12-year-old schoolchildren were enthralled with an account of this melancholy ghost. When invited to suggest a likely solution to the mystery, their imaginations were set alight. Here are two of their stories.

(1) Once upon a time, long, long ago, there was an old inn standing on a hillside. The innkeeper and his wife had a little girl whose name was Ellen, and they lived together happily until one day when

Ellen's mother died with a fever. That was why a stepmother came to live there. Ellen was afraid of her stepmother because she was always cruel and spiteful.

Before one or two years passed, her father died as well. So poor Ellen was left all alone with her stepmother in the lonely old house. Sometimes when she was naughty her stepmother put her in the dark, cold cellar and locked the door. Ellen cried bitterly because she was frightened and hungry.

One winter, when the hills were white with snow, the little girl was locked in the cellar all day long and throughout the night. At last her crying was too faint to be heard.

Another day passed before her stepmother opened the door. But Ellen was lying at the bottom of the stairs, and she was not crying or moving any more. That night, when the inn was quiet, the cruel woman buried her body under the cellar floor. Nobody ever found her there for everyone thought she had gone away. Whenever winter came and the wind blew from the hills her ghost was heard crying in the dark, and knocking on the cellar door. No-one went down to the cellar once the lamps were out.

100 years passed by, and one day the house was burned down in a fire. That was when Ellen's bones were found and buried in the churchyard. And then the ghost went away for ever.

(2) One day, in ancient times, the Celts and the Romans fought a battle on a hillside. Many men were slain and their bodies lay all about. They were buried together in a big grave and a mound of stones was built there to mark their resting place.

A young girl lost her sweetheart in the battle, and every day she came to the burial mound to grieve for him. All day long she would stay at the graveside crying bitterly. She could not live without him and died there of a broken heart. After a time her bones were found among the stones on the mound. But her ghost would never leave the hillside.

Centuries passed by, and eventually the grave was lost when a road was made and a tavern was built where the warriors had been buried. But the ghost of the broken-hearted girl remained to haunt the tavern. Her voice was heard weeping in the cellar.

In 1937 the house was burnt down. Now some trees have grown above that place. And if you walk along the road on a quiet night you will hear the leaves whispering and a voice crying softly.

The Visitor

A very old tale is remembered of a farmer who once lived alone at a farmhouse on a desolate stretch of moorland in the county of Brecknock. The long-house was built of a shaly stone and stood hidden in the shadows of the Brecon Beacons.

It was a winter evening. The wind sighed through the shutters at the window and the cattle were lowing in their stalls. The old man was sitting before the fire. Once his day's work was done he was alone with his memories, for no-one ever came to visit him. And every night he longed for company. Wistfully he looked into the hearth and whispered to the fireplace. 'Yn wir, fe rown hyd yn oed

122

fy enaid, er mwyn cael cwmni i siarad â mi.' (Indeed, I would give even my soul for someone to talk to.) He stirred the smouldering peat and said over and over again, 'Ie, fe rown hyd yn oed fy enaid.' (Yes, I would give even my soul.)

No sooner had he finished muttering to himself than the wind stopped sighing and the cattle were silent. All the house was still. Then, after a little while, the horses were heard whinneying in the stable and an icy draught put a bright glow in the fire. The lantern swayed from side to side, throwing shadows about the room. Upstairs, footsteps crossed the bedroom floor, and a voice, calling his name, reverberated around the house. 'Joseph ... Joseph,' it murmured in the chimney and through the shutters.

Terrified, the old man looked about him, listening to the ghostly sounds. Who could it be, he wondered, for one moment the voice came whispering from the stairway, the next from the darkness of the passage.

According to the story, the haunting recurred at intervals all through that night. Weird noises were heard, and then, when everything seemed quiet again, the voice returned, sighing first in one corner and then another. The old farmer lifted the latch, but the door would not open. The shutters, too, clung together at the window frame as though someone was holding them fast. At last he could stand it no longer. Trembling with fright, he fell to his knees and muttered a prayer that he might be alone again.

When the night had passed, the door opened freely and the first light of dawn was showing over the hilltops. Whoever had come to keep the old man company had gone away with the darkness.

The Ghost of Whitford Sands

From the village of Llanmadoc in the Gower Peninsula the road swings north through Cwm Ivy and then peters out, leaving a pathway through an open area of National Trust. Beyond a short stretch of moorland lies a wood and the dunes of Whitford Burrows overlooking the beach.

No-one can tell when the strange tales of Whitford Sands* began, but it is well known that from time to time after nightfall the beach is haunted by the sound of animal hoofs which come galloping across the sands. They approach from the direction of Broughton Bay, two miles to the south-west, grow to a thundering crescendo, and then fade in the distance.

Over the years various stories have been told to explain the origin of this ghostly phenomenon. They range from prehistoric times to the 19th century.

During the last of the great Ice Ages the Bristol Channel was a wide river valley, supporting plant and animal life to feed the cave dwellers whose primitive homes faced the meagre warmth of the Ice Age sun. In Gower (Longhole and Paviland Caves) the bones of man and beast have been unearthed by archaeologists. Many animal species survived the severe conditions of that time. There are some folk who believe that the phantom footfalls of a mammoth or woolly rhinoceros still flee from the hunters' spears over the Whitford Sands. Others say that the ghosts of the Silures, the Iron Age tribe whose ruined forts still stand on Llanmadoc Hill, charge down to the shore to repel Roman invaders. Some speak of the spirits of Viking raiders, or conquering Norman lords from long ago.

The following tales were related by some old inhabitants of Penclawdd and Llanmadoc.

(1) One day, many years ago, some women of Penclawdd had been

* The village of Penclawdd is well known throughout Wales for its cockles. Women in sea boots, flannel gowns and fringed shawls over their shoulders gather the cockles along the northern shore of Gower and on Whitford Sands. They take them back to their village in sacks by donkey and cart. There they are cooked and sold in the markets of Swansea and Llanelli.

gathering cockles on Whitford Sands. Their sacks were filled and loaded on the carts. They were leading their donkeys toward the Burrows when they were startled by a sound like galloping hoofs approaching from Broughton Bay to the south. A moment later there appeared, charging across the beach, an enormous mammal with a thick woolly coat. It thundered toward them, its feet cutting into the sand, its head hung low. A fearsome horn protruded above the snout. Snorting furiously, the beast charged among them. The women were terrified. Carts were upturned; donkeys were gored and lay twitching in the pools left by the ebbing tide. For a long time the beaches along the coast of North Gower were deserted.

In the months that followed, the beast appeared again and again, running amok in the marshes of Llanrhidian and along the Whitford Sands. From which time and place it came no-one knew.

Now there lived at that time in the hamlet of Cheriton a 'Knowing One' – an old woman well skilled in witchcraft. One evening, just at sunset, she was seen passing through the woodland at Whitford Burrows on her way to the beach. Her shoulders were bent, her grey hair awry, and a shawl was wrapped about her.

Near the water's edge she scratched a large circle in the firm sand with the horn of a ram, and inside she arranged Dead Man's

Fingers* and wreaths of purple Laver Weed.† Then she was seen to mouth a silent incantation.

After a while the moon grew bright and the sound of heavy footfalls was heard. Then the woolly beast appeared, charging toward her. The old woman stood her ground, chanting some weird spell above the crash of the waves.

The moment the beast set foot inside the circle it became strangely docile. Its snorting ceased and it stood there quietly, staring at the old woman.

'Be gone, Beast of Hades!' she cried. And in words of enchantment she banished the pitiful creature from the shores of Gower, never again to be seen on the marshes of Llanrhidian or the Whitford Sands until the tide had turned 100,000 times. Immediately the spell was cast, the beast faded to a misty shape and then vanished altogether. The sound of its hoofs became faint in the distance.

But this happened early in the 19th century and the beast's years of penance are almost over. Any day now he may reappear somewhere between Bluepool Corner and Whitford Point.

(2) About 150 years ago there lived in the village of Llanmadoc a farmer who was well known for his ungodly ways. After the death of his widowed mother he decided to take a wife to look after the farmhouse and tend the cattle. He chose for his bride a girl from the village of Llangennith. Although she was not beautiful she brought along a handsome dowry which he accepted gladly.

For a while she learned to tolerate his angry moods, but as the months passed by she became more and more afraid of his fiery temper. Then one night he returned home from a local tavern much the worse for drink. His wife was in bed asleep, and no supper had been prepared for him. Angrily he awakened her. Voices were raised and a bitter quarrel ensued. It is said that in his fury he beat her so cruelly that she fled from the house in terror, making her way over Whitford Burrows. In a drunken rage he staggered in pursuit. But the dunes were swathed in darkness and he searched for her in vain. It is believed that for a long time she hid in the woodland above the sands.

At first light the farmer saddled his grey stallion and set off,

* Branch-shaped sponges which cover the rocks at lower water mark.
† This seaweed is cooked and eaten as laverbread, a local speciality.

determined to bring her back. He searched the slopes of Llanmadoc Hill and then headed north toward the dunes.

At Hills Tor he spurred his horse to a gallop when he saw her on the shore near Broughton Bay. As the thundering hoofs drew close she screamed and fell to her knees. But he drove his horse straight on, trampling her into the sand. Again and again he turned about and rode over her. Before sunset her body had been washed by the tide and lay sprawled among the seaweed.

For the rest of his life, and for more than 100 years after his death, the cruel farmer of Llanmadoc has known no peace, for his ghost still gallops over the Whitford Sands.

Tales of the Whitford spectre are many and varied, but to this day a ghostly presence haunts that lonely shore.

One night during the long summer of 1976 a party of young folk from a nearby camping site were enjoying a barbecue on the beach. Their singing and guitar strumming stopped suddenly when an unusual sound, like the rumble of thunder, was heard. But the sky was clear and the moon bright. It grew louder, now like the galloping hoofs of a horse. It seemed to pass right through them and then fade away in the distance. Wide-eyed, the youngsters looked at one another, and a dog which had lain at their feet slunk off over the dunes.

A Haunted Ship

A strange tale is told of an old Irish mail-boat which was commissioned as a surveying vessel in Her Majesty's navy midway through the 19th century. H.M.S. *Asp*, as it was called, was being refitted at Pembroke Dock when the ghost which haunted her first made its presence known.

A dockyard worker who went aboard early one morning was startled to hear a voice whispering to him on the after deck. He described it as a strange chanting sound, reminiscent of the mythical sirens who lured sailors to their death on the rocks.

'A soft, enchanting voice,' he recalled. 'Like waves washing the shore.'

The captain of the vessel, a Commander Aldridge, smiled when the incident was reported to him. But stranger happenings were to follow and a brief account of some are recorded in the ship's log.

14th August, 1851: '... Mysterious noises were reported coming from an unoccupied after cabin. This incident was investigated by the bosun, but no cause was found. The cabin was subsequently locked ...'

23rd September, 1851: '... Further sounds of knocking on the inside of the after cabin door have been heard by several members of the crew. The cabin was unlocked and thoroughly searched. No explanation was discovered ...'

3rd December, 1852: '... Seaman Ferris has been charged with deserting look-out duty. During a summary hearing it was alleged that the figure of a woman appeared on the after deck, beckoning and pointing below deck. On medical examination the accused was found to be sober but emotionally disturbed ...'

During the summer of 1853, while the ship was lying at Lawrenni in the Cleddau, the steward was alone below deck when he was alarmed by the voice of a girl sobbing. The sound seemed to follow him wherever he went. Terrified, he fled from the ship, never to return.

The captain could not dismiss these weird occurrences as the superstition of seafaring men for even he admitted to awakening in a cold sweat one night when a hand was placed on his forehead in the darkness of his cabin.

Time and again both he and members of the crew experienced the sound of a whispering voice, a peculiar rapping within the locked cabin, and once a shrill scream in the dead of night.

Then in the winter of 1857 the vessel put into Pembroke for repairs. During the first night in harbour a dockyard sentry swore that the figure of a woman appeared on the after deck of the *Asp*, and then came ashore toward him. He dropped his musket and fled to the guardhouse where the spectre seemed to pass right through him. Another sentry fired at the ghost as it passed along toward the old Pater churchyard nearby. That was the last time it was seen or heard, for never again was its presence reported aboard the ship.

Following this remarkable train of events, Commander Aldridge traced the history of the ship and listened to accounts of her voyages around the coast of Ireland before it was commissioned. It was then that he heard the gruesome story of a murdered girl whose body was discovered in an after cabin. Her identity and the circumstances of her death were never known.

A Haunted Place

If you travel from Swansea to the north-west along the new highway
you will pass by, and perhaps never notice, many places with
memories of long ago – just as someone might stroll through a
churchyard without a thought for the folk buried there.

One such place is a stretch of common known as Garngoch,
skirted by Penllergaer Woods on its east side and the winding
stream of Afon Llan to the south. Garngoch (The Red Hilt of the
Sword) is said to be named after a bloody battle fought there in
Roman times, and a mound on the common is believed to be the
remains of a burial ground. The skirting woodland, called
Penllergaer Woods (The Chief Place of the Legion), is also of
Roman origin, and was well known as a local beauty spot and a
popular haunt of lovers.

So this lonely stretch of common, fringed with woodland, holds
countless memories of days long gone. Tales are told of ancient
battles on the common, and of tragic love affairs in the wood.

Here are some of the stories which were gathered there.

One evening a long time ago a traveller was crossing the common at Garngoch. He had passed Bryn Dafydd on his journey south when a sudden breeze whispered over the ground. It grew in strength until the ferns swayed from side to side and the sound of it moaned across the common. His horse shied, whinnied momentarily, then jogged on its way. In a little while the air was still again.

When he came to the banks of the stream at Afon Llan the traveller dismounted to water his horse. He was surprised to notice that the animal's hoofs were red with blood. He examined each leg in turn, but found no wound. So he walked his horse through the stream and at once the blood stains were gone. But the water flowed on in clear, sparkling ripples. A few minutes later, refreshed and back in the saddle, the traveller went on his way.

A tinker on his travels one night trundled along the path over the common. The lantern hanging from his horse-drawn cart swung to and fro and its light made pools of green on the ground. All the while his pots and pans clanged and tinkled as he went by. A blanket was wrapped around his shoulders to keep out the cold east wind.

Then, before he had gone very far, a strange thing happened. For no accountable reason the pots and pans behind him on the cart rattled louder still, like the sound of drums beating and swords clashing. In a moment it seemed that the frightful noise of battle was all around. Voices were heard crying out in pain and anger.

The tinker was rigid with fright as he stared around in the darkness. But nothing stirred on the common except the ferns beside the path swaying in the wind.

The ghostly battle raged for a little while longer and then faded away like a fast train passing by. The tinker took a whip to his horse and the lantern on his cart swung wildly as he hurried away.

WOODLAND TALES

One day, while walking through the woods at Penllergaer, an old man and his granddaughter came to a glade where bluebells were growing. There they saw a fair-haired girl among the flowers. Her head was buried in her hands and at first it seemed that she was kneeling in prayer. But then she was heard weeping softly. It was strange that although they could see her as clear as day, the bright rays of sunshine shone right through her misty shape.

The little girl said to her grandfather, 'Tad-Cu, paham maer'r ddynes yn wylo?' (Grand-dad, why is the lady crying?)

'Mae hi'n cofio dyddiau trist flynyddoedd maith yn ôl, cariad,' (She is remembering sad days of long ago, darling,) her grandfather replied.

Then he took his granddaughter by the hand and together they went on their way into the shade of the trees.

A grey mist was hanging over the trees when a young man came helter-skelter through the lodge gates at the edge of Penllergaer Woods. There was a look of fear in his eyes and he ran like the wind.

It was not until he was sitting before a fire in a local inn with the nightmare far behind him that he told of his hurried flight through the evening mist.

In the quiet of the woods he had heard following close behind what sounded like the echo of his footsteps. He had stopped to listen and the footsteps came on, accompanied by a strange animal sound. But there was no-one to be seen on the path behind him. For a while he had been too afraid to move, but then he had turned and fled with

someone – something – in close pursuit. There were no longer
footsteps at his heels, but the marks of hoofs tore the grassy path and
a frenzied snort was almost upon him.

When he had passed the lodge whatever had been following him
was gone. Only his footsteps were heard on the open road.

'Lle'r Diafol ydyw!' (It is the place of the Devil!) the young man
exclaimed.

There are a number of stories concerning the lonely stretch of
woodland at Penllergaer. Most are of days long past and are almost
forgotten by the old folk who live thereabouts. But perhaps strangest
of all is a quite recent tale.

A traveller from West Wales was motoring south-east along the
A48 when, somewhere in the vicinity of Penllergaer, he
inadvertently turned off the main road and lost his way. For a while
he drove on, looking along the roadside for a signpost to guide him.
It was a dark night with rain flowing steadily down the windscreen.
The road was deserted.

Presently the car's headlights shone on a solitary figure walking
ahead. The traveller stopped and asked the stranger if he could
direct him to the main west road. It was a young man who stood
there at the roadside. His hair hung over his shoulders and an

upturned collar hid his face. Without a word the stranger opened the door of the car and sat down beside the driver. Then, with not even a sideways glance, he pointed ahead and the traveller drove on.

He continued along the road for a mile or two, without turning to the left or right, passing alongside a church and a wood. All the while the stranger sat silently beside him. When they reached a place called Cadle Mill he got out of the car, for now the road ahead led to Swansea and the east. The mysterious stranger whom he had come upon in the darkness walked off into the night. With a whimsical smile the traveller carried on his way.

Two days later he was returning to his home in Carmarthen. Taking the main Carmarthen road out of Swansea, he soon found himself speeding along a wide dual carriageway. The road was strangely unfamiliar. Surely this was not the route he had travelled on his way east? His thoughts returned to the rain and the darkness and the stranger he had encountered a short while ago.

At a local service station he made enquiries about the alternative route through Penllergaer, and it was there that an explanation made him strangely ill-at-ease.

'There was a through road once, a couple of years ago,' he heard the attendant say. 'It went past the church and down by the woods. But it is closed now.'

The Scarecrow

Siôn Dafydd was a tough old man, close to 70. He lived alone in a shack a few miles into the hills, not far from Rhandir-mwyn. It was a dingy place, barely furnished; a palliasse stuffed with straw, a fireplace, and a few sheep skins scattered on the dirt floor. When the weather was fine he spent much of his time wandering among the farms around Llandovery, and sometimes was seen as far north as Tregaron. There was no mistaking Siôn Dafydd as he tramped the hills dressed in his shabby coat and peaked cap, with a muffler tied about his neck.

Now and again he repaired dry-stone walls for the shepherd folk, and late on in summer he helped the farmers gather in their crops. Then, with a few shillings jingling in his pocket, he would make his way to the local taverns where he would while away the evening drinking mugs of ale and singing lusty songs. There were times when he would set off for home, staggering along the mountain paths, only to break his journey in some sheltered dell and fall asleep among the heather.

In the winter time he rarely ventured far from his shack. But sometimes after dark he could be seen skulking around in the moonlight with a dead sheep slung over his back or a fowl hung limp at his side. Then, night after night, the smell of roast mutton would waft from his chimney and the sound of his raucous singing would tumble down the hillside, for he was seldom without a bottle of spirits to keep out the chill night air. There was hardly a farmer or an innkeeper along the banks of the Tywi who didn't know of Siôn Dafydd's drinking and bawdy song.

One winter a shepherd who passed by on his way to the hills noticed that day after day the shack was quiet with no smoke in the chimney. When he knocked the door and looked inside he found the old man lying on the floor. He had been dead for some time.

There was no-one to mourn old Siôn Dafydd. He was buried in a pauper's grave. His shack fell to ruin and his miserable possessions were left there – all except his shabby clothes. These were taken away by a neighbouring farmer and wrapped about a scarecrow which stood among his crops. With the torn cap, crumpled jacket

and a muffler stirring in the wind it looked more like Siôn Dafydd than a sack of straw staked out in the field.

The spring passed and summer wore on and the old man was forgotten. Then one evening two farm-hands were returning home from the village tavern. As they made their way along the road they caught sight of the scarecrow silhouetted in the moonlight. For a while they stood there peering at it over the hedge. Then, terrified, they ran off toward their cottage as fast as their legs would carry them.

'Hen Siôn Dafydd oedd yn sefyll yno!' they said to their folk. 'Fe ddechreuodd ganu ac fe aeth ei lais yn adsain drwy'r dyffryn!' (It was old Siôn Dafydd standing there! He began singing and his voice went echoing through the valley!)

STRANGE OCCURRENCES

Canwyll Corph

There is a traditional belief among the old folk of West Wales that a shining omen – a spectral candle – portends death or tragedy. The Canwyll Corph (Candle of the Corpse), it is said, appears along funeral paths or over the place of impending disaster. Some say that St David himself asked in prayer that his people be given this sign so that they could prepare themselves for death, and to strengthen their faith in the hereafter.

Far to the east, where the heather uplands slope down to the valleys, there are tales of the Tylwyth Teg (Fairy Folk) who appear in the form of a funeral procession surrounding the black veiled bier. They too foretold a person's death. With uncanny accuracy they followed the path along which the corpse was to be carried to the graveyard.

There are many tales of the Canwyll Corph and phantom cortege.

In the days of long ago, when life was simple and leisurely, such tales were numerous. In the hurly-burly of the 20th century they are rare – but not unknown.

PHANTOM CORTEGE

The village of Penally stands on the western coast of Carmarthen Bay, with Caldy Island lying two miles to the south.

One evening an old man of the village was walking home along the moonlit road in the vicinity of the church. He had passed by the churchyard when he noticed a dark shape at the roadside moving toward him. As it drew near he saw in the moonlight that a funeral procession was approaching, with the coffin at its head carried by six bearers.

In all his three score years at Penally he had seen many funerals, but had never known of a corpse being interred after nightfall. Stranger still was the eerie silence of it all, for the mourners passed by without even the sound of a footfall. And although he recognised many of his neighbours among them, no-one glanced his way as he stood there with doffed hat and head bowed in reverence.

The cortege moved toward the church. Then, for some unaccountable reason, it left the road and crossed over the hedge and headed toward the boundary wall of the churchyard. In a short while it had gone out of sight. All night long the old man lay awake pondering over the mystery.

So the next morning he told the vicar of this strange occurrence. But he could offer no explanation.

'How odd,' the vicar remarked with an unheeding smile.

The old man spoke first to one and then another of the mourners whom he had recognised in the moonlight. But each one wore a startled frown and hurried on his way. After a while he spoke no more of his vision on the moonlit road.

The winter was long and severe with biting winds sweeping across the bay. Soon after the beginning of the new year the old man fell ill, and before St David's Day he was dead.

His funeral procession left the farmhouse and proceeded toward Penally churchyard. Six neighbours carried his coffin and the cortege trudged along through a thick carpet of snow. When they approached the church they found that a deep snow-drift blocked the road, whereupon they crossed over the hedge at the roadside and made their way around the boundary wall of the cemetery.

WRAITH AT ABERYSTRUTH

An extract from the diary of a scholarly man, Edmund Jones, of the parish of Aberystruth in the old county of Monmouth, tells of a strange happening in the village midway through the 18th century.

One evening a Mr Howard Prosser, Curate of Aberystruth, saw a funeral coming down the church lane toward the church. Knowing of a man from the north of the parish who had lain critically ill, he assumed that he had died and that the corpse was being borne to its resting place in the cemetery.

He put on his band to perform the burial rites and hastened to meet the procession. He did not think it strange that he recognised no-one in the cortege for he knew that they came from the borders of Breconshire.

He put his hand to the black cloth of the bier and took out his prayer book as was the custom in those days. But in a moment all vanished, and to his astonishment he discovered that instead of the bier's veil, he held in his hand nothing but the skull of a dead horse.

FALLING STAR

Just a mile or two to the north of the village of Penally along the Carmarthen Bay is the town of Tenby, with its 15th century boundary walls and the keep of a 13th century castle standing as relics of its past. A few of the old folk remember strange happenings of long ago which were never recorded in the town's history. One such tale of years gone by is of a spectral candle, a Canwyll Corph.

One night a 15-year-old girl, in service at a country house overlooking the bay, lay awake in her bed. The curtains were open and through her bedroom window she saw a thousand stars sprinkled in the sky. As she lay there watching them twinkle, she caught sight of a falling star. Instantly she closed her eyes and made a wish, for according to an old superstition if the trail of light had not vanished before she opened her eyes again, then her wish would come true. After a fleeting moment her eyes opened wide and she was surprised to discover that the streak of light was still falling through the sky.

Instead of burning out in just a few seconds it grew bright and glided low over the bay. Then it moved toward the window, hovered there a while, and then entered the room, finally coming to rest at the foot of her bed. It shone like a shaft of sunlight.

The girl screamed with fright and everyone in the household came rushing to her room. But in another moment the light went dim and vanished. That was the last night she spent under her master's roof, for she was too afraid to remain there.

Many weeks passed by. Then one day the master's wife was taken ill and died quite unexpectedly. Her body was laid to rest in the spare bedroom which had been occupied by the young servant girl.

THE DEVIL'S DISCIPLE

Old Harries Cwt-y-Cadno (Fox's Tail) lived in a farm of that name near the banks of the river Tywi on the outskirts of Carmarthen. He was feared by most folk, for it was said that he talked with the devil, cast sinister spells on his enemies and generally led a life of sin.

'Fe aiff y diafol â fe,' (The devil will take him away,) folk used to say, 'a 'i losgi yn nhannau uffern.' (and will burn him in the fires of hell)

Then one winter morning Harries Cwt-y-Cadno was found dead in his bed. His Gwylnos (Wake Night)* was a drunken orgy, a night of wild revelry. But his funeral was pitifully sparse, with scarcely enough mourners to carry his coffin to the cemetery.

As they were approaching the graveyard along a narrow roadway, the bearers were startled when suddenly the coffin became almost weightless. Just then a ghostly trail of candles appeared along the roadside, flickering in the dusky light.

Nowadays none of the local folk ventures over that lonely stretch of road once nightfall approaches. Since the funeral of Harries Cwt-y-Cadno that late afternoon long years ago, no-one has seen the phantom lights. But, it is said, even on a balmy evening there is always a chill breeze at the place where Satan snatched an old disciple.

* see Wake Night at Dolranog.

143

A Strange Omen

It was half-past 10 one autumn night when old Mrs Dalamore was looking through the window of her terraced cottage in a mining village of the Afan Valley. There she spent most of her time, with the curtains opened wide, watching – always watching.

From the pale light of dawn to the fiery sunset, she looked from east to west. She saw the sheep on the mountain, the milk cart trundle along the road, women off to the corner shop, children at play. There was little that escaped the watchful eye of old Mrs Dalamore.

There was no moon that night, but myriad stars twinkled overhead. Then an unusual sight attracted her attention. Moving slowly over the mountain side was a trail of lights glowing in the darkness. They swayed gently from side to side and travelled along the mountain path. Every minute they came closer, and before long they had dipped down into the valley and were moving along the village road. She saw them glimmer as they passed by her window

144

and finally come to rest outside the home of Llewellyn Williams, hovering there at the doorway. Apart from the glow of the lights nothing else was to be seen, and in another moment they went dim and vanished.

'Good Heavens!' the old lady muttered to herself, for she could scarcely believe her eyes.

The next night, and many times throughout the autumn, when nightfall came she looked toward the mountain. But not once did the lights reappear – not until one night the following summer.

At half-past-10, just as before, they were seen moving over the mountain path and then descending along the road to the village. As they passed by her window she heard the crunch of heavy boots and saw the blackened faces of colliers as they trailed by, the glow of their Davey lamps swaying to and fro and flickering upon them. At their head were four men carrying a stretcher on which lay the body of young David Williams who had been killed when pit-props had collapsed underground.

Lamps were lit in neighbouring cottages and folk stood in their doorways as the tragic procession walked past. It came to rest at the door of Llewellyn Williams.

Two nights later, on the eve of young David's funeral, lights were again seen around the doorway. Many of his workmates had come to pay their last respects, for the next afternoon they would be back at work on the coal-face. Their Davey lamps glimmered and the sad harmony of Dafydd y Garreg Wen (David of the White Rock) drifted through the valley.

Footprints in the Snow

One afternoon, more than 100 years ago, the young daughter of an innkeeper from the village of Bryncethin sat idly gazing out of the window. It was dusk. A carpet of snow lay on the ground and clung to the rooftops. For a while she watched the snowflakes swirl around the window pane. Then, close by, the strangest sight appeared before her eyes.

'Edrych, dad; edrych draw fynna!' (Look, father; look there!) she cried, pointing to the forecourt of the tavern. And there, resting on the mounting stones,* was a coffin. It lay there as clear as day.

There was not a living soul to be seen although there were footprints all about leading to and from the front door. But when the innkeeper peered through the window there was only an empty courtyard, a lamplighter across the way and drifts of snow driven against the steps. The coffin and the footprints had vanished as mysteriously as they had appeared.

Many weeks passed by. The folk of Bryncethin visited the tavern

* During the last century mounting stones were a common sight at taverns. They were steps about two feet high which were built in the forecourt to help travellers climb into the saddle.

as usual, but the strange incident was never mentioned, for the villagers were superstitious about such things.

Later that winter a farmer from farther along the valley died, and his body was to be interred at Llansantffraid Churchyard. On the day of the funeral a heavy fall of snow covered the ground and the cortege trudged wearily along the road to Bryncethin. When they came to the tavern they laid the coffin to rest on the mounting stones in the forecourt. Then the bearers and the scant party of mourners went inside for a while to warm themselves before the blazing log fire. After taking a tot or two of whisky to keep out the biting wind, they set off again on their journey to the churchyard.

If ever you pass through the Ogmore Valley, going north toward the Rhondda, a few miles beyond Bridgend you will come to the village of Bryncethin. And there, outside the Mason's Arms, you will see the mounting stones standing today as they did more than a century ago.

Ceffyl Dŵr*

Along the southern coasts of Wales there are many tales of the Ceffyl Dŵr. Descriptions of this strange, romantic creature vary from place to place and from person to person, but most tell of a winged wraith, graceful as an Arab steed with flowing mane, white as the driven snow. It haunts the beaches, the dunes and the rocky cliffs, never far from the billowing sea, and moves above the ground as swiftly as the wind.

Although it glows as brightly as moonlight in the darkness, the Ceffyl Dŵr is not entirely a creature of the night, for it has been seen at dawn and dusk and faintly in the midday sun.

Usually it appears as a silent spectre, but sometimes it has been known as a creature of substance, performing deeds of rescue and even of cruel vengeance. There are tales of fishermen clutching its flowing mane when fierce winds have dashed their boats upon the rocks. Many a villain, attempting to capture the phantom horse, has been attacked by flashing hoofs or carried high above the shore and plunged into the sea from the back of a raging beast.

Here is one such haunting tale of a Celtic Pegasus.

* Phantom Steed.

The village of Oxwich lies on the south-west coast of the Gower Peninsula. One summer evening an old fisherman from the village had been out in the bay with his grandson. It was long after dark when they moored their boat by lamplight. Their journey home took them across the beach and along a narrow path leading to the church.

After trudging on wearily for a while, the boy had the strange feeling that someone or something was following them. Looking over his shoulder, he saw what appeared to be the luminous figure of a white horse prancing along on its hind legs. It made no whinnying sound and its hoofs were silent as they trampled upon the path. He drew his grandfather's attention to the ghostly presence, and together they watched it move toward the churchyard gate.

The apparition passed through the gate without difficulty and then just seemed to thin out and vanish. For a minute or two they stood in silence. Then the grandfather said, 'Come along, it's way past our bedtime.'

The ghostly creature was not seen again in the village for many years. Then one night the rector who was passing through the churchyard after evensong saw a misty animal form drifting among the tombstones.

The three witnesses to this strange occurrence now lie buried there, and memories of the weird churchyard visitant are buried with them.

Haunted Hills

On the moorland lying to the south-west of the Preseli Hills there are not many folk who remember the white-washed farmhouse which stood on the slopes of Mynydd Morfil and overlooked Ty-rhyg Wood. Today the few remaining stones lie hidden among the heather, and there they have lain for more than 100 years.

Long ago it was the home of a shepherd who lived there with his wife and two young sons. One evening he was out on the hills as usual when the strangest thing happened. The sun was going down over Mynydd Cilciffeth and to the east, cumulus clouds heaped above the summit of Foel Eryr. Shafts of light from the setting sun laid a golden path across the sky. The clouds darkened and a sudden wind ruffled the heather. Then a distant sound like thunder rolled over the hills.

What appeared next made the shepherd blink with astonishment. From beneath the base of the clouds, which now masked the peak of Foel Eryr, a legion of soldiers came marching over the horizon, their shields and spears catching the glint of the falling sun. Chariot wheels rumbled, and a drum beat measured the army's steady advance.

In a place close by, the shepherd's sons stood in awe, unable to believe their eyes.

'Look! Look there!' they called out, pointing to the skyline.

From the opposite direction a horde appeared from over the top of Mynydd Cilciffeth, some afoot, others on horseback, rushing toward their foe.

As the silver-edged clouds raced by overhead, two armies met in combat. Horses pranced. Swords and shields clashed. Spears flashed. The angry cries of battle were heard as warriors charged forward, some being slain and trampled underfoot. The conflict was fierce and bloody.

For more than an hour the fighting raged on Mynydd Morfil. Then lightning streaked across the sky, and for an hour more torrential rain swept over the hills. The shepherd and his sons found shelter in a craggy dell.

The clouds had gone and the moon was growing bright when, at last, they made their way home.

Throughout that summer many farmers spoke of the sudden storm which plunged the hills in darkness and swelled the valley rivers. They well remembered the violent peals of thunder and streaks of light, but of the beating drums and the warrior figures appearing from over the horizon, nothing was ever heard.

Nowadays, if you walk over the moorland along the slopes of Mynydd Morfil or Mynydd Cilciffeth, you will find it has changed little over the years. The sheep still roam among the heather and morning mists often swirl in the valleys. There are no legions on the skyline, but perhaps their ghosts haunt the burial mounds* that lie on the hilltops.

---

* Mynydd Cilciffeth, Foel Eryr and Mynydd Castlebythe surrounding Morfil in the north of Pembrokeshire are all crowned with burial mounds, centuries old.

A Vision at Treffgarne

The old farmhouse was nestling on the slopes of the Great Treffgarne Mountain, overlooking the Western Cleddau river which rises in the Preseli Mountains and flows south through the old county of Pembrokeshire. On a fine day, when the sun had raised the veil of mist from the hills, one could see the legendary Maiden Castle* and the site of ancient buildings, once inhabited by the Romans.

It was on such a day that Sarah, a wizened old lady, sat in the window looking down into the valley. Ever since the days when she was young she was known as a fortune-teller, for she told of many things that came to pass; the failure of crops, the coming of storms, births and deaths. She foretold them all.

As she sat there at the window, a strange sight appeared to old Sarah.

'Well, good heavens! Bless my soul!' she breathed, for it was so unusual she could scarcely believe her eyes.

That evening, when her son came in from the fields, she told him what she saw. She described a number of wagons travelling fast through the valley below the house. '... one behind the other, with no horses pulling them, but the sound of their hoofs galloping along.' She believed that the leading wagon was on fire, for '... clouds of smoke came pouring from its roof.'

In the middle of the last century the railway was extended westward to Pembrokeshire. Workmen made cuttings in the Treffgarne Valley when it was planned to extend the line to the coastal towns of Fishguard and Goodwick in the north. But for some reason the engineers abandoned this plan and took the line instead to Neyland in the south. Then, some years later, they reverted to their original plan and extended the line to Fishguard.

So today, if you are ever journeying to the north of Pembrokeshire, where the railway meets the ferry to Ireland, you will travel through the Treffgarne Valley. And, going along 'in fast

---

* Maiden Castle was never a building, but an outcrop of volcanic rock whose silhouette bore the likeness of a ruined castle.

moving wagons following one behind the other, with no horses pulling them', you will hear the wheels rumble on the track like the sound of galloping hoofs. You will pass over the Western Cleddau river and perhaps see Maiden Castle in the distance, silhouetted against the sky.

The old farmhouse no longer stands on the slopes of the Great Treffgarne Mountain, but the strange vision of an old lady is remembered to this day.

As for Sarah herself, it is said that she died late in the 18th century – more than 20 years before George Stephenson first introduced steam locomotive power.

Wake Night at Dolranog

To the south of Carningli Common in the new county of Dyfed lies the little village of Dolranog, nestling among the lonely hills and moorland of the Gwaun Valley. On winter nights, when folk gather around the hearth, the story is told of an uncanny incident which occurred there more than a century ago. It happened one night at a Gwylnos.*

An old farmer from the village had at last come to the end of his days of wickedness. Throughout the village, and beyond, he was known for his ungodly ways.

'Repent, and cast out the devil!' the minister had implored as the sinful man lay on his death bed. 'Follow the paths of the Lord, or perish in the flames of hell-fire!'

But with a mocking laugh the old man had died, unrepentant.

* A Gwylnos or Wake Night was held on the eve of a funeral in West Wales during the last century. Brief lamentations and much merrymaking was the usual custom among the country folk.

154

Now he lay cold in his coffin, and his lips were curled in a faint grin.

The candles were lit and neighbours came from the hills to his farmhouse on the fringe of Pen-rhiw Woods. The Gwylnos continued well into the evening, with little lamentation and much revelry and merrymaking. The sound of the harp and bawdy song filled the kitchen and drifted toward the woods.

Suddenly galloping hoofs were heard approaching. The singing stopped and eyes peered through the window out on to the moor. There were no horses seen on the hillside, but the galloping came on, the hoofs now clattering on the stony path. Then the door burst open and the candles were blown out by an icy draught, uncommon on a summer night. For a while there were murmuring voices and darkness.

Several moments passed in silence. Then the sound of the galloping hoofs was heard again, noisily at first outside the doorway, and then growing faint across the moor. Relatives and neighbours muttered one with another. Then the candles were re-lit and the revelry continued.

The night drew on, and at last the Gwylnos came to an end.

155

Before leaving, two nephews from Cwm-mawr farther down the valley went into the room where the corpse lay, to look for the last time on the face of their departed uncle. And there they made a startling discovery. The coffin was empty and the body of the old man had vanished. It was never found.

Folk say that the following day the coffin was filled with stones and buried in the churchyard.

Cwn Annwn*

In the days of long ago, when roads were unlit and the moonlight threw shadows from the trees and hedgerows, village people told of the strange sights they had seen and the curious sounds they had heard as they passed through the countryside. Some of the most terrifying tales have been of the cwn annwn.

There have been various descriptions of these ghostly hounds, but generally they are believed to be ferocious animals, often hunting in packs. Although they were never known to attack anyone, their baleful eyes and awesome baying struck fear into the stoutest heart. At the sound of their approach villagers ran indoors and were afraid to venture out until morning light, for the cwn annwn were known to be creatures of the night. Sometimes, above the howling of the hounds, the cracking of a whip was heard and the laughter of their master, said to be Satan himself, as he rode behind on his black steed, urging them to run faster.

The cwn annwn, peculiar to the counties of Wales, have long remained a mystery. According to legend, the spectral hounds are earthbound spirits who, because of their ungodly lives, have been transformed and doomed to haunt in darkness.

The following tales of the cwn annwn are remembered from a time long before modern roads and street lighting banished the phenomenon from the country lanes and moonlit highways.

(1) Many centuries ago a Norman baron, Robert Fitzhamon, after several bloody battles, eventually subdued the Welsh in the low-lands of Glamorgan. When the fighting was over and his captive lands secured, life held no excitement for him. As the months passed by he tired of his lonely existence, so he went on a journey to his native Normandy. When he returned to South Wales he was accompanied by a voluptuous lady whom he had known in the past and who would now help him while away his wearisome days.

Throughout the county of Glamorgan she was admired for her beauty. But her fair appearance hid a heart of steel. Her selfish ways

* Hounds of Hades.

157

were well known, and her cruel deeds were spoken of in whispers. Her favourite sport was hunting. There was nothing she loved more than riding her black stallion with the hounds, mercilessly tracking down her prey. She rode as well as any man and was once heard to vow, 'If hunting is forbidden in Heaven, then I shall stay forever in Hades!'

For many years she pursued her ungodly ways. Then, one autumn day, she met her untimely end while chasing with the pack across the downs. Her horse shied near a cliff-edge and she was thrown to her death.

It seems that hunting was forbidden in Heaven and that, true to her word, she stays forever in Hades, for there have been many times after nightfall when the cwn annwn have been seen loping across the moor. According to the tales, they are accompanied by an old hag who howls and screams in chorus with the braying hounds. Known to the frightened villagers as 'Gwraig o Uffern' (Woman of Hades) she charges through the night on a swift black steed, dressed in a scarlet, hooded cloak. With sunken eyes and sallow cheeks she bears no resemblance to the beautiful lady of Normandy. But, as folk always say, 'Ni all guddio ei henaid hyll.' (She cannot hide her ugly soul.)

(2) The little seashore town of Laugharne on the south coast of Dyfed provided a haven during much of his adult life for the Welsh poet, Dylan Thomas. He once described it as a 'far, forgetful ... place of herons ... castle, churchyard, gulls, ghosts ... mysteries ... pubs ... rain ... and human, often all too human, beings.' By some folk it is remembered, too, as a place of the ci annwn, for early in the 18th century a solitary spirit-hound appeared there on a number of occasions.

One winter's evening, long years ago, a fisherman was making his way home from the river. Darkness was falling and a cold wind whistled through the trees at the roadside. He walked past the castle walls and farther on came to a crossroads. There in the dusky light he saw what appeared to be a large white dog lurking in the shadows. It stared at the fisherman, baring its teeth and growling menacingly. The frightened man backed away as the beast lunged forward. Then he turned and fled, with a ferocious snarling close at his heels. A short distance from the crossroads he stumbled and fell. Then, lying helpless on the ground, he could only watch in terror as the hound stood over him.

'Duw a'm helpo!' (God help me!) he cried.

Then, with a plaintive howl, and much to the amazement of the poor fisherman, the beastly shape grew faint and vanished.

The crossroads was the scene of many strange occurrences, often involving the appearance of the ci annwn. No explanation was ever found except that, true to legend, the spectral hound proved the harbinger of death, for in those days it was usually at a crossroads where murderers swung on the gibbet.

OCCASIONAL TALES

The Murder Stone

It was late at night when two men strolled unsteadily through the
churchyard at Cadoxton on their way home from a local inn.

'Duw mawr pa beth a welaf draw? Diwedd a braw i'r holl fyd ...'
(Great God what do I see beyond? An end of things created), they
sang to the tombstones standing beside them in the moonlight.

At first their raucous voices drowned the cry that came from the
darkness. But then, from the marsh below the church, there came
again and again the scream of someone in terror. A little while later
the silhouette of someone appeared from behind the church. It ran
among the graves and through the gates of the churchyard toward

the row of cottages standing on the hillside nearby.

The mysterious figure had emerged from the darkness and then vanished again before the echo of the Welsh hymn they were singing had faded away.

Beneath the branches of a yew tree in the churchyard of the parish church of Saint Catwg in the village of Cadoxton there stands an unusual tombstone. It is now weathered with age and the inscription grows faint. On the stone is written:

> 1823. Murder. This stone was erected over the body of Margaret Williams, aged 26, a native of Carmarthenshire living in service in this parish, who was found dead with marks of violence upon her person in a ditch on the marsh below this churchyard on the morning of Sunday, 14th July, 1822.

> Although the savage murderer escapes for a season the detection of man, yet God hath set His mark upon him, either for time or eternity. And the cry of blood will assuredly pursue him to a certain and terrible but rightful judgement.

At the foot of the stone, half hidden among the ivy, is added:

> Canys nyni a adwaenom y neb a ddywedodd myfi biau dial, myfi a dalaf, medd yr Arglwydd.
> (For we know who it was that hath said: vengeance belongeth unto me, I will recompense, saith the Lord)

The tombstone, it is said, was placed in such a position that its fearful epitaph faced the row of dwellings on the hillside where the suspected perpetrator of this crime lived. And before many months had passed an inhabitant from one of these cottages boarded a cargo vessel at Swansea docks and began a new life overseas.

The Devil's Hiding Place

For as long as anyone can remember there have been mysterious stories of treasure hidden somewhere along the north-west coast of Gower. Since days long past folks have searched through marshland and among the coves, but always their quest for gold was fruitless. The secret hiding place of the treasure was never discovered.

Then one night a cleric from the village of Llanrhidian retired to his bed at the end of a tiring day. As he lay asleep a strange dream came to him. In his dream he found himself walking through a dusky wood, and then descending a path to a cove on the north shore. There, stretching before him, he saw imprints in the sand where the cloven feet of an animal had trod. The footprints led him toward the rocks and disappeared in the depths of a cave. It was dark inside, but in his dream a lantern glowed and he heard in heavenly tones the refrain of an old Welsh lullaby. Its haunting melody echoed through the cave. Almost at once a cleft in the rock opened like Aladdin's treasure house to reveal a black cavern beyond. The lantern passed through the stone doorway and a glint of gold shone out.

When the cleric awoke in the quiet of his room he was filled with awe at the revelation that had come to him. He tingled with excitement and there was a spark of greed in his eyes.

That evening, just after sunset, he set off with his man-servant to retrace the journey he had made in his dream. The shadows were lengthening but he well remembered the way. His servant was beside him, carrying a small bardic harp and a lantern to light their way.

They hurried through the wood and along the winding path. Then, step by step, they followed the footprints in the sand. Inside the cave there was no sound but for the whisper of the ripples falling on the shore.

'Play!' the cleric commanded, and then, 'Play on!' he cried when his servant's harp brought the music of his dream and the cleft began to open.

Inside the cavern heaps of gold strewn on a rocky shelf glittered in the lamplight. The cleric's gasp of astonishment brought his servant

163

hurrying to his side. But in a moment their chuckles of glee changed to cries of alarm, for with the treasure hunters inside the cavern and the music stopped, the stone door closed behind them.

And now, it is said, if ever you find that lonely cove and walk along the sand when the water is calm, you will hear a haunting tune coming from the darkness of the caves. There two ghosts of long ago are trying to escape from their golden tomb.

A Mystery at Brandy Cove

Brandy Cove is a small inlet on the south coast of Gower between Pwlldu Head and Caswell Bay. It lies hidden beneath the cliffs and steep gorse-strewn banks, and in years gone by it was a favourite haunt of smugglers for it is one of the most secluded beaches around the shores of South Wales.

About 60 years ago strange tales were told of a haunting at Brandy Cove. On many a moonlit night during the 19th century small boats had been seen bobbing among the silver-tipped breakers as the smugglers had stolen ashore. Often they had crossed the sandy beach and made their way to the caves at the foot of the cliffs. But it was not the seafaring men of the last century that haunted the cove for more than 40 years. It was the ghostly voice of a woman.

Late one afternoon in the autumn of 1920 a young couple were climbing the steep path which led up from the beach. Darkness was falling when they were startled to hear the voice of a woman screaming. Her screams echoed through the caves. There was nothing to be seen in the dusky light. Warily they retraced their steps and approached the caves. For a long while they listened there, but the voice was heard no more. At length they made their way home.

Some days later a fisherman from the village of Murton described a similar experience. He was walking along the water's edge when, above the sound of the waves washing the shore, there came a shrill cry from somewhere beyond the shadow of a cave. The beach was deserted. He listened for a minute or two longer and then made all haste up the path to the cliff-top.

In the years that followed, this strange phenomenon recurred from time to time. In the neighbouring villages of Pennard, Bishopston and Newton tales were told of frightful screaming piercing the silence of the cove. And although sceptics spoke of the wind whistling through the caves never a soul ventured near Brandy Cove after sunset.

The following accounts, described in old newspaper cuttings, may well throw some light on this mystery:

October, 1919. There was much concern among the residents of south-east Gower over the disappearance of Mamie Stuart, an attractive young woman who had left her native Sunderland to begin a new life in South Wales. Before settling in the village of Newton she resided for a time in the town of Swansea with a marine engineer named George Shotton. He was later to appear before the Assizes charged with bigamously marrying her at South Shields Registry Office in March, 1915, and was sentenced to 18 months' imprisonment. Following police enquiries it was learned that Mamie Stuart had last been seen at Newton on November 12, 1919 by the landlady of the Ship and Castle (now the Newton Inn). A thorough search was made at Ty Llonwydd, the house in which she had lived, but there was no trace of the missing woman, apart from articles of clothing and a few personal belongings. And the police failed to trace the whereabouts of George Shotton since his release from prison. The mystery aroused the interest of reporters from a number of the leading daily newspapers, and there followed a spate of anonymous letters claiming that Mamie Stuart had been seen in various places throughout the country. Enquiries continued well into 1920, and Mamie's disappearance was investigated by officers of Scotland Yard. But finally, on July 10, 1920, the police abandoned their search, concluding that there was no evidence to suppose that the missing woman was dead. So the mystery of Mamie Stuart was forgotten, until one day some 40 years later.

November 5, 1961. On this Sunday morning three young men from the village of Bishopston went exploring in the caves at Brandy Cove. Their excursion down an old lead mine air shaft led them to a gruesome find. At the foot of the shaft they passed through two layers of rock which had a narrow fault, and this brought them into an ante-chamber. At the end of the chamber was a tunnel which probably led into the old mine workings. This was blocked by boulders. When these were moved, the explorers were confronted with what they thought at first was solid wall. But closer examination showed it to be a slab of stone about three inches thick which had been placed on end, resting on the boulders. And behind the slab they discovered a human skeleton.

The police were notified, and the party returned to the mine shaft. Working under the direction of the police, who were unable to enter the opening, the potholers retrieved the skeleton from its tomb.

Forensic tests proved that the remains were of a woman about 25-years-old, and that her body had lain there for more than 30 years.

Two rings, found among the bones, were later said to be similar to those worn by Mamie Stuart. The verdict ultimately given at a coroner's inquest was that she had been murdered by person or persons unknown, and that her body had been concealed in a disused mine shaft shortly after her disappearance in 1919.

In later years George Shotton was traced to a cemetery in Bristol, where he had died in 1958 in his 78th year.

The bones of the north country woman were blessed and buried in the churchyard at Bishopston where they lie to this day. And, strange to say, since the winter of 1961 it is only the seagulls that scream beneath the cliffs at Brandy Cove.

The Highwayman

Early in the 19th century the A40 was the stagecoach route from London to the port of Fishguard in West Wales where the ferry-boat crossed to Ireland. At the English border the road swings south-west through the counties of Gwent and Powys. From Abergavenny to Brecon it follows the path of the river Usk, with the Black Mountains to the east and the Brecon Beacons to the west.

Long ago this 20-mile stretch of roadway was the haunt of a notorious highwayman who waylaid travellers on their journey through the valley. From time to time folk were confronted by a horseman who suddenly appeared in their path. Victims were robbed and sometimes murdered, but the highwayman was never brought to justice. Although the villain's identity was not proved, a gentleman from the village of Crickhowell was regarded with much suspicion, for he was rarely about after nightfall, and on moonlit nights his piebald mare had often been seen carrying a masked rider along the valley road.

The years passed by and the gentleman of Crickhowell prospered. At length his nocturnal escapades came to an end. For the rest of his life he lived in a fine house and became well respected in the village. It is believed that he died in about 1850.

There was at that time in the south-eastern counties of Wales a belief in the magic of the 'Sin Bearers'. These were usually miserable outcasts who were engaged to join the cortege on the day of the funeral. On the coffin were laid bread and ale and a silver coin. The outcast was invited to eat the bread and drink the ale, and so took into himself all the sins of the deceased. Then the departing soul would rest in peace, never to haunt after death.

The 'Sin Bearer' engaged on this occasion was said to be a gaunt old man with a sallow complexion and long grey hair. As the cortege assembled outside the house, the simple-minded peasant consumed the bread and ale, accepted the silver coin and so, according to superstition, took upon himself the sins of the gentleman who was laid to rest in the cemetery at Crickhowell.

Some years later, when the old peasant was himself in his grave, strange tales were told in the villages along the valley. Many a time,

when the moon was bright, a ghost would appear on the roadway at different places between Abergavenny and Brecon. Travellers would come upon a masked rider on a piebald mare, who emerged from the woodland and peered into their carriage. He was described as a gaunt old man with sunken eyes whose long hair shone silver in the moonlight.

An Enchanted Stream

Wales has been described as the land of wells, for hidden among its hills and crags are more than 1,000 to which some belief or legend is attached; wishing wells, healing wells, haunted wells, and countless stories of dirgelaidd dwr (mysterious waters).

Here are two such tales of the enchanted stream of St Teilo, from the old county of Carmarthenshire.

(1) To the south of the road from Mynydd-y-Garreg to Four Roads in the parish of Kidwelly stands the ruins of an old chapel. There, in a quiet ravine below the chapel, flows the dark waters of Pistyll Teilo* (the stream of St Teilo).

Its healing powers were well known in the parish, and many folk came there to bathe their bruised and crooked limbs in the water.

One day two men, one with blue scars from his work on the coal-face, the other with a lameness in his leg, decided to test the magic properties of the pistyll. They left the road and descended a rugged path in the rocks which led down into the ravine. When they reached the bottom they found it cool and silent there, although along the way skylarks had been singing in the afternoon sun. Now there was only the faint sound of the water as it rippled by.

They rolled their trousers up to their knees and chose a spot where the water ran deep. An odd sight they looked beside the stream, sitting together on the mossy bank, with spindly legs dangling in the water. The pistyll licked their limbs with an ice cold tongue. But, steadfast, they sat with wry faces until their ailing parts were blue and numb.

After a while they were startled by a haunting sound. A voice, like the whisper of waves on a distant shore, called to them. They looked about with staring eyes. There was no-one. Then the voice came again, clearer than before.

* Pistyll Teilo is mentioned in A.D.H. Coxe's *Haunted Britain*, as is Ffynnon Fair, a spring in a marshy field at Kidwelly, where the Virgin Mary is believed to have died while visiting places where Christ is said to have been as a young man. And '... where she fell a spring rose ...'

'It is cold and lonely waiting for the sons of William,' it said in their native tongue. And echoes whispered back from the rocky face of the ravine, '… sons of William … sons of William.'

'Tylwyth Teg!' (the Little Folk!) muttered the lame man. But his companion well remembered the little folk's fear of water.

'Ysbrydion!' (Ghosts!) he replied.

Then quickly they gathered in their arms bundles of boots and clothing and scrambled up the path to the roadway, where they arrived pale and breathless, with fresh bruises to heal.

(2) It was getting dark when the old man passed the chapel ruins. He pulled on the reins and stopped for a while to give his horse a rest. Then he lit the lantern hanging beside him on the cart and climbed down to stretch his legs. He would be home before nightfall. His faithful collie loped off toward the old chapel with his nose to the ground.

Presently the dog came slinking back; the horse whinnied and reared in the shafts. Then the old man, too, was strangely disturbed, for a voice was calling from the dusky light below the ruins. Like a sudden wind moaning through the ravine and then drifting away in the distance, it sighed, '… sons of William … of William … William …'

To this day the old folk of the district never pass along the road above the ravine after nightfall, because they fear the ghostly voice

171

which calls from the bottom of the cwm. Perhaps one day the 'descendants of William' will be discovered and the mystery of the ghostly voice will be solved. And if ever they immerse their aching limbs in the chill water of Pistyll Teilo, the voice will be silent forever.

The Devil's Bridge

One of the most famous Welsh beauty spots lies to the east of
Aberystwyth, the university town overlooking Cardigan Bay. If
you turn off the main highway to North Wales on the A4120 you
will come to the wooded gorges of the Rheidol Valley and Devil's
Bridge, which spans the foaming waterfalls of the River Mynach.
Nearby is the well-known Jacob's Ladder, a flight of 113 steps which
descend to the river at the bottom of the gorge.

At different times since the Middle Ages three bridges have been
built to carry a roadway over the Mynach. Today they stand one
above another. The second dates from the 18th century, and in 1901
this was replaced by the present bridge. Historians assume that the
lowest, stone, bridge was built in the 12th century by monks of the
Cistercian abbey at Strata Florida, but legend says that it was built
by the Devil.

Long ago there was no bridge at all spanning the Mynach. At that
time an old widow lived in a cottage near the river bank. For
company she had only her Welsh terrier, and for a meagre living she
relied on her cow whose plentiful yield of milk was churned into
butter and sold to the villagers at Pont Erwyd.

One morning at milking time she wrapped her shawl around her
shoulders and, with her dog beside her, went out into the field where
her cow was always put to graze. But the cow was nowhere to be
seen. She had strayed farther up-stream where the water was
shallow and had found her way to the south side of the Mynach. It
was dusk when the old woman saw the animal again, but
throughout a day of thunder-storms the river had swollen and now a
torrent of water separated the widow from her cow. 'Beth yn y byd
gallaf wneud?' (What in the world can I do?) the old woman cried.
'Fe grwydra'r fuwch nes i ddi ddiflannu am byth.' (The cow will
wander off and be lost forever.)

Just then she heard a voice calling to her from the other side of the
river. Standing there in the shadows was someone dressed in the
robe and cowl of a Cistercian.

'Marged ... Marged,' the monk called above the din of the

173

waterfall. 'Don't be distressed. I will build a bridge across the water.'

Old Marged had heard of miracles performed by holy men and in her desperate plight she was glad to accept help from anyone. 'How can I repay such a kindness?' the credulous widow replied.

The stranger came to the edge of the river bank. His robe touched the ground, and beneath the hood his dark features showed, with eyes that burned like fire. 'I ask only one thing in return. My reward shall be the first living being to cross the bridge.'

His voice had a deep, ringing tone which drowned the noise of the rushing water. Marged's dog slunk forward and lay at her feet. A moment later a flash of lightning lit up the sky and then, magically, a stone bridge appeared, spanning the gorge. The stranger stood on the south side, his arms outstretched. 'Come, Marged,' he called. Then he came forward, and his voice grew louder still, echoing through the Rheidol Valley. 'Marged, cross over the bridge!'

But the poor old woman was too terrified to move. She watched from the opposite bank as he approached step by step, commanding her to walk toward him. Then, with hackles up and teeth bared, Marged's faithful dog ran at the monk, tearing at his robe and revealing the cloven hoofs which had been hidden by the flowing garment. There was a further flash of light followed by a shriek of rage. Then the stranger and the dog vanished in a cloud of blue smoke. They were never seen again.

It is said that old Marged lived on for many a year in her cottage near the river bank. Often she was seen leading her cow to pasture, and whenever she crossed the stone bridge of the Mynach falls she shed a tear for the faithful companion who saved her soul from the Devil.

Three Tales of Dirgelaidd Dwr*

THE WISHING WELL

A few miles from Llandeilo in the old county of Carmarthen stand the ruins of Carreg Cennen. The castle was built in the 13th century on a steep crag of limestone beside the River Cennen. An underground passage beneath the ruins ends in a cave, and there, in a depression in the rock, lies an old wishing well. The magic powers of the water are believed to have originated long ago and are well known to all the local folk.

There was once a farmer from the village of Llangadog who lived a simple life among the hills. Day after day he worked in the fields, tilling the soil or reaping the harvest. And when dusk was falling he drove his cattle home from pasture. But always his head hung low and his heart was heavy. After dark he sat with his wife in their lamp-lit room. He loved her well enough, but as the years wore on his sadness grew, for he had watched the sparkle fade from her eyes and her hair become tinged with silver. She was no longer the girl he had loved in his youth. He knew that time moved on as surely as the waters of the Tywi and that only magic could hinder its passing.

So one day, on his way home from market at Llandeilo, he stopped his pony and cart beside the ruins of Carreg Cennen Castle. He made his way along the underground passage and peered into the dark pool which sprang from the rock. Only a trickle of water disturbed the silence when he whispered his wish to the spirit of the well.

'O pe bai fy ngwraig yn ieuanc ac yn deg eto.' (If only my wife were young and beautiful again.) And then, since it was the custom, he dropped into the well a rusty-headed nail which had lain buried in an oak beam for three winters or more.

It was late in the afternoon when the farmer arrived home, and someone was waiting for him at the doorway. A beautiful girl with deep, blue eyes and soft, golden hair was standing there. Imagine his joy and amazement when he recognised the girl he had fallen in love with all those years ago.

* Mysterious Waters.

176

For a while they lived happily, just the two of them together in a lonely farmhouse. But before winter came he was sad again, for she tired of the old farmer with his care-worn face and weary step. Folk say that she went far away from Llangadog with a handsome young man whom she met at the fair in Carmarthen.

PWLL CYFAREDDOL

Tales of the Pwll Cyfareddol (Pool of Magic) have been told in many corners of the world; in the Mountains of Mourne, the Scottish braes – even as far away as the Cameron Highlands which overlook the jungles of Malaya. Legends go back into prehistoric times, and there is evidence of a cult of wells and springs in the Celtic Iron Age. Although the places and names are different, the mystery is always the same. Folk believed that the Pwll Cyfareddol cast an enchanting

spell on anyone who touched the water.

The following account is from somewhere among the hills to the south of Tregaron. It concerns a young girl, the 12-year-old daughter of a Cardigan shepherd.

One day she set off into the hills with her collie, in search of some sheep which had strayed beyond the dry-stone walls. Far away she wandered, for she was seen on a craggy hillside many miles from home. Folk say that she made her way down into a dell where wild flowers grew on the banks of the Pyll Cyfareddol.

Dusk had fallen, but the girl and her dog did not return to the farm. And although the hills were searched by torchlight and throughout the days that followed, over hill and cwm and every shady copse, they were never seen again.

NICKY NICKY NYE

Nowadays, tales of bogies and water-ogres are rare, and it is perhaps only children who take them seriously, for such superstition began to fade at the turn of the century. But long ago young children were taught to fear these demons, to frighten them away from dangerous lakes and rivers. Such tales were prevalent near the south-eastern borders of Wales.

Long ago the name Nicky Nicky Nye was well known and feared by the folk of Monmouthshire, for he was described as an evil old man with withered face and sunken eyes. Should anyone stray near stagnant pools all green with weeds, or river banks where the water rushed by, then the gnarled fingers of Nicky Nicky Nye would stretch up from the depths and drag them to him. It was there that he lurked, always watching, always waiting.

One summer's evening, so the story goes, a young girl who lived beside the woods at Llantrisant wandered off to the banks of the River Usk where she spent some time playing alone. Then, presently, she ran screaming from the water's edge, and there was a look of terror in her eyes. For a while she cried and trembled, but at length she told of a hand which came out of the river and clutched at her clothing. Although no-one, but an old woman of the village, believed her story, her frock was torn and there were marks on her leg like the scratches of sharp finger nails. And for the rest of her life the waters of the Usk filled her with dread.

A warning rhyme about the bogie of the river is still remembered by the old folk of Monmouthshire:

> Nicky Nicky Nye
> He pulls you down,
> Underneath the water,
> To drown, drown, die.